THE MAILBOX®

REAL-WORLD Comprehension Practice

Skill-Building Activities to Help Students Read Real-Life Texts

- **Making Inferences**
- **Drawing Conclusions**
- **Determining Cause and Effect**
- **Comparing and Contrasting**

- **Identifying Main Idea**
- **Finding Supporting Details**
- **Determining Purpose**
- **Using Text Features**

Written by Shawna Miller and Kim Minafo

Editorial Team: Becky S. Andrews, Kimberley Bruck, Karen P. Shelton, Diane Badden, Thad H. McLaurin, Debra Liverman, Marsha Erskine, Sherry McGregor, Amy Payne, Karen A. Brudnak, Sarah Hamblet, Hope Rodgers, Dorothy C. McKinney

Production Team: Lisa K. Pitts, Pam Crane, Rebecca Saunders, Jennifer Tipton Cappoen, Chris Curry, Sarah Foreman, Theresa Lewis Goode, Clint Moore, Greg D. Rieves, Barry Slate, Donna K. Teal, Zane Williard, Tazmen Carlisle, Marsha Heim, Lynette Dickerson, Mark Rainey

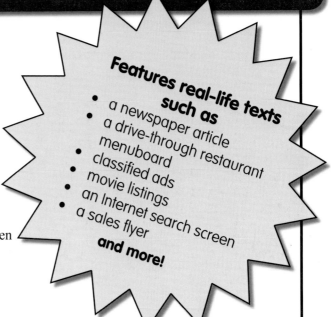

Features real-life texts such as
- a newspaper article
- a drive-through restaurant menuboard
- classified ads
- movie listings
- an Internet search screen
- a sales flyer

and more!

www.themailbox.com

©2006 The Mailbox® Books
All rights reserved.
ISBN10 #1-56234-698-9 • ISBN13 #978-1-56234-698-0

Table of Contents

School Supply List 4

School Rules 7

Product Ad 10

Classified Advertisements 13

Newspaper Article 16

Sales Flyer 19

Movie Listings 22

Magazine Cover 25

Game Rules 28

Assembly Instructions 31

Recipe 34

Drive-Through Menu 37

Food Nutrition Label 40

Summer Camp Brochure 43

Web Site Homepage 46

Internet Search Screen 49

Weather Map 52

Mall Directory 55

Weekly Schedule 58

Table of Contents 61

Telephone Book 64

Encyclopedia Page 67

Dictionary Page 70

Comic Strip 73

Multiple-Choice Response Sheet 76

Answer Keys 77

How to Use

This resource provides 24 real-world reading selections based on what kids encounter every day, such as movie listings, a sales flyer, or an Internet search screen. Each selection is accompanied by two follow-up practice pages for assessing students' comprehension of the selection. The reading selections can be used with individuals, small groups, or the whole class.

To use, simply make a copy of a real-world reading selection for each student or pair of students, or if desired, make a transparency of the page. Read aloud the selection or have your students read it independently. Then have students complete one or both of the follow-up practice pages.

Real-World Reading Selection

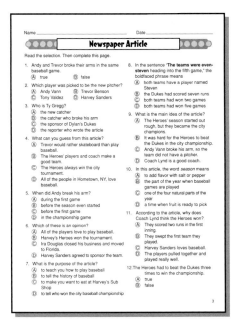

Practice Page 1
Assesses students' comprehension using a multiple-choice format

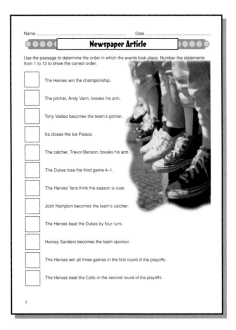

Practice Page 2
Assesses students' comprehension with an open format, such as short-answer questions, drawing a picture, describing a situation, labeling a diagram, or completing a graphic organizer

Dillard School
Fifth-Grade Supply List

Welcome back to school!

Please write your name on all of your supplies. Use a permanent marker. This will help you keep track of your materials all year. Before you buy your school supplies, read the list of products that are not allowed. Also see the list of project supplies you will need later this year.

Except for items needed for projects later this year, be sure to bring your supplies on the first day of school!

- ☐ 3 packages wide-ruled notebook paper
- ☐ 5 pencils (#2)
- ☐ box of 24 crayons
- ☐ small pencil bag
- ☐ pair of scissors
- ☐ clipboard (optional)
- ☐ 3 glue sticks
- ☐ package of sticky notes—any color or size

- ☐ box of tissues
- ☐ backpack
- ☐ fine-tip black permanent marker
- ☐ 4 wide-ruled spiral notebooks
- ☐ 4 folders with pockets
- ☐ box of resealable storage bags
- ☐ $4.00 for a homework planner
- ☐ $4.00 for the classroom magazine

Additional Supplies

- October project supplies: poster board, box of colored chalk, large glue sticks, old magazines
- January project supplies: empty shoebox, buttons, yarn, bottle of school glue, colored pencils
- Restock these supplies often:
  - pencils
  - crayons
  - paper
  - glue
  - tissues

Items That Are Not Allowed

- mechanical pencils
  They can be nuisances and cannot be used for testing.

- rolling backpacks
  They can be tripping hazards.

- oversize binders
  They do not fit in your desk.

- college-ruled paper
  Wide-ruled paper provides more space for writing.

School Supply List

Read the selection. Then complete this page.

1. According to the list, which item is required?
   - (A) a box of markers
   - (B) a clipboard
   - (C) a pair of scissors
   - (D) blue sticky notes

2. What is true about both the spiral notebooks and the notebook paper?
   - (A) They must both be wide ruled.
   - (B) They must both be college ruled.
   - (C) Students will need to bring in more notebooks and paper.
   - (D) They are both optional.

3. Based on the list, you can conclude the following:
   - (A) Students will need more supplies during the year.
   - (B) Teachers prefer yellow sticky notes.
   - (C) Students do not need scissors.
   - (D) Students do not need to label their supplies.

4. What might have caused the school to ban rolling backpacks?
   - (A) Students do not like rolling them.
   - (B) They cost too much.
   - (C) They are easy to break.
   - (D) Someone tripped over one and got hurt.

5. Students do not need to buy clipboards.
   - (A) true
   - (B) false

6. The main purpose of this list is to
   - (A) entertain
   - (B) describe
   - (C) persuade
   - (D) inform

7. A student can wait until January to buy which of these supplies?
   - (A) colored chalk
   - (B) poster board
   - (C) buttons
   - (D) black permanent marker

8. Students must bring money to school to buy all of their supplies.
   - (A) true
   - (B) false

9. Why are students told to use permanent markers to label their supplies?
   - (A) The markers will last forever.
   - (B) The markers will remain at school.
   - (C) The marks made with the markers will not last.
   - (D) The marks made with the markers will last.

10. Wide-ruled paper has
    - (A) lines that are far apart
    - (B) lines that are close together
    - (C) rules for the class
    - (D) no lines

11. How might this supply list be organized to make it easy to use for shopping?
    - (A) Put the items in alphabetical (ABC) order.
    - (B) Put the items in groups by how many are needed.
    - (C) Group together items that are alike.
    - (D) Make the list into a paragraph.

12. Students must bring all project supplies to school before labeling them.
    - (A) true
    - (B) false

School Supply List

Use the selection to choose the correct answer.

1. Each student needs four spiral notebooks.   Fact   Opinion

2. Rolling backpacks should not be allowed at school.   Fact   Opinion

3. Homework planners cost too much.   Fact   Opinion

4. Fifth graders at Dillard School must use wide-ruled paper.   Fact   Opinion

5. Students may need more supplies during the school year.   Fact   Opinion

6. Glue sticks are harder to use than bottled glue.   Fact   Opinion

Choose one opinion from above. Do you agree with it? Tell why or why not. Include three reasons that support your opinion.

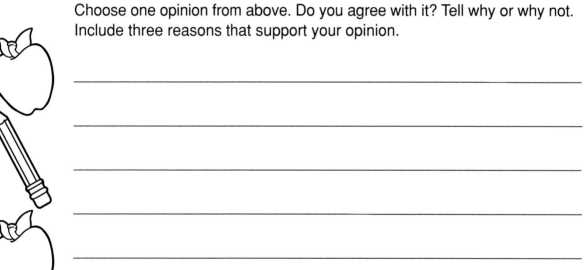

©The Mailbox® • *Real-World Comprehension Practice* • TEC60917 • Key p. 77

Orange Grove School District

Section One: Attendance Policy
Students must attend school daily to meet learning goals. Students need to be at school on time. It is also state law that children ages 5 through 17 must attend school.

Students may be excused from school for the following reasons:
- illness (A doctor's note will be required after three absences.)
- doctor or dentist appointments
- family emergencies
- special religious services or holidays

Students will not be excused from school for the following reasons:
- family trips
- babysitting

Any other absence must be approved by each school's principal.

Section Two: Reporting an Absence
To report each absence, call the school attendance line before school starts. Leave a message that includes the following information:
- child's name
- date of the absence
- reason for the absence
- parent's or guardian's telephone number

School Name	Office Phone Number	Attendance Line
Orchard Elementary	555-1234	555-1233
Redwood Elementary	555-1111	555-1112
Orange Grove Middle School	555-2222	555-2223
Orange Grove High School	555-3333	555-3331

Section Three: Makeup Work
Makeup work must be turned in within three days of each absence. Call the school office to request makeup work.

Page 2

Name _____   Date _____

School Rules

Read the selection. Then complete this page.

1. This selection is mainly about
   (A) unexcused absences
   (B) attendance rules
   (C) excused absences
   (D) schools' attendance lines

2. Which of these is not an excused absence?
   (A) dentist appointment
   (B) illness
   (C) doctor appointment
   (D) family trip

3. Who can approve a special reason for being absent?
   (A) parent   (C) teacher
   (B) principal   (D) student

4. Which school district has this policy?
   (A) Orange Grove School District
   (B) Orchard Elementary
   (C) Pecan Grove School District
   (D) Orange Grass School District

5. Where will you read about how to report an absence?
   (A) Section Two   (C) Section Four
   (B) Section Three (D) Section Five

6. Babysitting is an unexcused absence.
   (A) true   (B) false

7. This selection was most likely written for
   (A) principals   (C) children
   (B) teachers   (D) parents

8. According to the selection, why should students attend school?
   (A) to get good jobs
   (B) to earn awards
   (C) to meet learning goals
   (D) to get good grades

9. Students have _____ to complete makeup work.
   (A) one week   (C) two days
   (B) three days   (D) two weeks

10. If a student had to stay home to take care of his or her sister, the principal would approve the absence.
    (A) true   (B) false

11. If you attend Redwood Elementary, which phone number will you call to get your makeup work?
    (A) 555-1234   (C) 555-2223
    (B) 555-1233   (D) 555-1111

12. If an absence is excused, it is
    (A) babysitting   (C) not okay
    (B) a family trip (D) okay

Name _____ Date _____

School Rules

Use the selection to complete the outline below.

Topic: _____

    I. _____
main idea

        A. _____
supporting details

               _____
supporting details

        B. _____
supporting details

               _____
supporting details

   II. _____
main idea

  III. _____
main idea

Using your outline, write a letter to the students of Redwood Elementary.
Explain the school district's attendance rules.

Orange Grove School District

_____

_____

_____

_____

_____

_____

_____

_____

_____

_____

Hey Kids! Look at This Great Stuff!

B **CD** 96-page book and an audio CD
Ages 6–12

C Learn to type while you have fun.
Ages 8 and up

C Learn sounds, words, and more!
Ages 4–9

Save Big!

D Watch the best racecar drivers in action!
Ages 6 and up

CD Ten great patriotic songs for kids
Ages 4–12

CD **D** **B** Learn Spanish in six months with this award-winning kit.
Ages 9 and up

B **CD** Read about 50 amazing animals. Hear zookeepers tell about their adventures.
Ages 3–7

To Order:

By mail: Complete this form and return it with your payment to
Super Kid, Inc., P.O. Box 8080, Yourtown, NC 00051

Online: go to **www.superkidinc.web**

Title	Quantity	Price
_____	_____	_____
_____	_____	_____
_____	_____	_____
_____	_____	_____
	Total	_____

Ship to
Name _____
Address _____
_____
City _____
State _____ Zip Code _____
Phone Number _____

Kids, get permission from one of your parents before placing an order.

Name _____ Date _____

 **Product Ad**

Read the selection. Then complete this page.

1. What is the book *Dandy Dinos* probably about?
   Ⓐ dinosaurs
   Ⓑ pets
   Ⓒ reptiles
   Ⓓ dogs

2. Tara will teach you how to _____.
   Ⓐ sew
   Ⓑ type
   Ⓒ knit
   Ⓓ read

3. The only product made for a three-year-old is _____.
   Ⓐ *Phonics Fun*
   Ⓑ *Animal Adventures*
   Ⓒ *I Love America*
   Ⓓ *Race & Chase*

4. If you are looking for some songs to sing along with, try _____.
   Ⓐ *Learn Spanish*
   Ⓑ *Phonics Fun*
   Ⓒ *I Love America*
   Ⓓ *Type With Tara*

5. *Learn Spanish* and _____ are the only products with DVDs.
   Ⓐ *Dandy Dinos*
   Ⓑ *Race & Chase*
   Ⓒ *Phonics Fun*
   Ⓓ *Type With Tara*

6. A child must get a parent's permission to place an order.
   Ⓐ true
   Ⓑ false

7. How can you place an order for these products?
   Ⓐ over the phone
   Ⓑ by mail only
   Ⓒ online only
   Ⓓ by mail or online

8. If you buy the *Animal Adventures* set, which items will you receive?
   Ⓐ a book and cassette
   Ⓑ a CD-Rom and book
   Ⓒ a CD and a book
   Ⓓ a book and computer software

9. According to the ad, *Learn Spanish* can teach you Spanish in _____ months.
   Ⓐ 9   Ⓒ 12
   Ⓑ 6   Ⓓ 8

10. If you want to order an item by mail, what is the first thing you should do?
    Ⓐ Complete the form in the ad.
    Ⓑ Go to www.superkidinc.web.
    Ⓒ Mail your payment.
    Ⓓ Get your parent's permission.

11. The purpose of this ad is to get kids to _____.
    Ⓐ read more
    Ⓑ rent movies
    Ⓒ buy items in the ad
    Ⓓ search the Internet

12. Which of these statements is a fact about the ad?
    Ⓐ All of the products listed are great.
    Ⓑ Learning phonics is fun.
    Ⓒ Each item costs $5.
    Ⓓ Kids will love reading about animals.

Name _____   Date _____

Product Ad

Use the selection to complete the chart below. Then answer the questions.

Title	Price	Format				Description
		Book	Computer Software	Audio CD	DVD	
1. *Dandy Dinos*	$5	X		X		a CD and 96-page book about dinosaurs for ages 6–12
2. *Type With Tara*	$5		X			
3. *Phonics Fun*	$5		X			
4. *Race & Chase*	$5					
5. *I Love America*						
6. *Learn Spanish*						
7. *Animal Adventures*						

8. If you do not own a DVD player, which products should you not buy? _____

9. Which product might a racing fan buy? _____

10. Why do you think *Type With Tara* is offered as a computer program instead of a book? _____

Classified Advertisements

Sporting Goods

Takoma 2005 Mountain **Bike**
(New 26" x 2.25" tires)
Like new, aluminum frame
$125 or best offer (obo)
Call 123-555-0154 for more
information

BMX **Bike** 2005 with
steel pegs
New 20" x 2.0" tires
Steel frame, great condition
$325 obo
(123) 555-0121

Ten-speed **Bike,**
includes helmet
Low miles, great condition
Aluminum frame
$650 obo
Call 123-555-0153

Proswing
Metal **Baseball Bat**
Adult weight
$100 obo
(123) 555-0168

GOLF CLUBS w/bag
6 irons, 2 woods, putter
$400 obo
progolf@123.web

Ballflight Big Eddie
Golf Driver
Lightweight, great condition
$660 obo
(123) 555-0182

Andrews **Kayak**
FOR SALE—like new
$425
Call 123-555-0164

Folding **Ping Pong Table**
Good condition
$485 obo
ping@pong.web

POOL TABLE w/accessories
Good as new
$375 obo
Call 123-555-0101

SAILBOAT
Just serviced
$750 obo
Call 123-555-0125

EZ Ride **Scooter**
Good condition
Call 123-555-0192

Girl's **Ice Skates**
Like new
White—Size 6
(123) 555-0160

Adjustable **Inline Skates**
Men's—Size 10
$60 cash only
Call 123-555-0188

Snorkeling Gear
Includes mask and snorkel
Never used
$60
(123) 555-0150

Swoosh **Snowboard**
Great condition
Contact
snow@wintersports.web

Surfboard
Used once
$200
Call 123-555-0164

Camping Dome **Tent**
2 person
$125 obo
(123) 555-0167

Tetherball Pole
FOR SALE
Ball included
$50
Call 123-555-0163

Trampoline
Pads included
Like new
$150
bouncing@trampolines.web

Treadmill—Runner 85
Low miles, 220V
$750
(123) 555-0129

Name _____ Date _____

Classified Advertisements

Read the selection. Then complete this page.

1. Which of the following items is available in good condition?
   - (A) Proswing baseball bat
   - (B) EZ Ride scooter
   - (C) golf clubs with bag
   - (D) tetherball pole

2. How much are the sellers charging for the Big Eddie golf driver?
   - (A) $400
   - (B) $100
   - (C) $660
   - (D) $425

3. Based on the ads, how are the ping-pong table and pool table different?
   - (A) Both tables are in good shape.
   - (B) Both owners can be contacted by phone.
   - (C) The pool table is more expensive than the ping-pong table.
   - (D) The pool table comes with accessories.

4. What would most improve the ad for the girl's ice skates?
   - (A) the skates' price
   - (B) the number of times the skates have been worn
   - (C) the phone number
   - (D) the owner's name

5. What conclusion can you draw from the ad for the tetherball pole?
   - (A) It includes a red ball.
   - (B) The seller will accept $25.
   - (C) A buyer can call for more information.
   - (D) The tetherball pole is new.

6. The mountain bike and the BMX bike both have aluminum frames.
   - (A) true
   - (B) false

7. What is the purpose of a classified ad?
   - (A) to entertain
   - (B) to sell something
   - (C) to evaluate the products
   - (D) to sell more newspapers

8. What does the phrase *or best offer* (obo) mean?
   - (A) The seller wants more money.
   - (B) The buyer can pay any amount for the item.
   - (C) The buyer must pay the price in the ad.
   - (D) The seller might accept less money for the item.

9. In the ad for the tent, what does *2 person* mean?
   - (A) Two people will fit in the tent.
   - (B) Two people are trying to sell the tent.
   - (C) It takes two people to carry the tent.
   - (D) The tent can only be set up by two people.

10. What might you substitute for *just serviced* in the sailboat ad?
    - (A) recently damaged
    - (B) needs repairs
    - (C) just painted
    - (D) recently repaired

11. According to the selection, every ad must include each item's price.
    - (A) true
    - (B) false

12. According to the selection, classified ads are usually sentence fragments.
    - (A) true
    - (B) false

Name _____ Date _____

Classified Advertisements

Use the selection to compare and contrast the three advertised bikes.

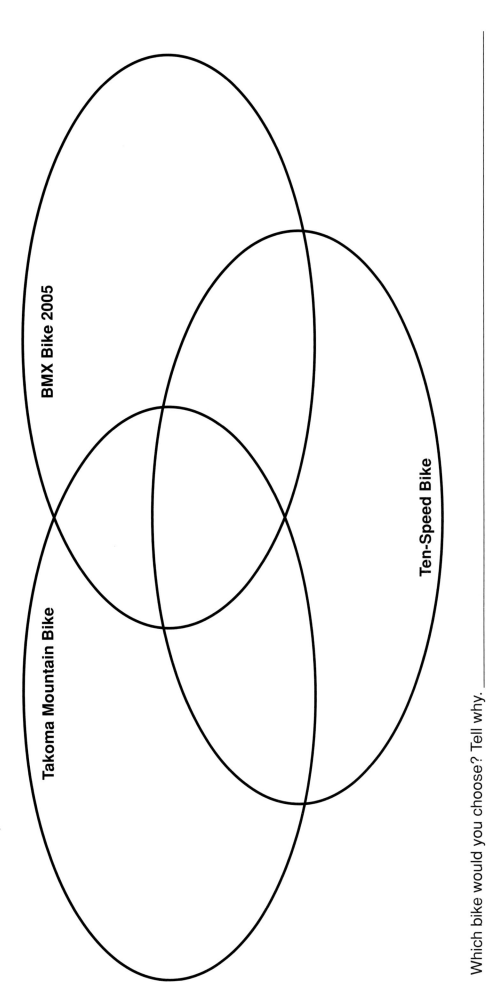

BMX Bike 2005

Takoma Mountain Bike

Ten-Speed Bike

Which bike would you choose? Tell why. _____

_____

Heroes Are New Hometown Baseball Champs

By Ty Gregg

HOMETOWN, NY—Harvey's Heroes are the new city champs. Dylan's Dukes gave the Heroes four hard games. But the Heroes won the fifth game with no trouble, cinching the title.

It was a rough season for the scrappy team. Ira's Ice Palace sponsored the team for the last ten years. When owner Ira Douglas closed the Palace in March, the team lost its sponsor.

"I hate to do it, but I'm moving to Florida. I'm tired of ice," Douglas said.

It looked like the team's season was over before it had even started. Then Harvey Sanders, owner of Harvey's Sub Shop on Main Street, stepped in. He agreed to sponsor the team.

"I've been looking for a local team to sponsor," Sanders said. "I love baseball!"

The team looked strong in its first game. But in the fifth inning, ace pitcher Andy Vann broke his arm. One week later Trevor Benson, the team's catcher, broke his arm doing a flip on his skateboard. Many fans thought the season was over.

Coach Mike Lynd gave Tony Valdez the nod to pitch and called on Josh Hampton to catch.

Valdez and Hampton have been working together ever since.

"I had to shuffle a few other players, but I've got a great group of kids here. I knew we had a winning lineup," Coach Lynd said.

In the playoffs, the Heroes swept the first team they played. They won three straight games against the Bulldogs. The second round was a bit tougher. The Heroes faced the Colts in four hard games. It took the Heroes two extra innings in the fourth game to defeat the Colts.

Then the Heroes faced the Dukes in the final round. The Dukes hadn't lost a game all season. The Dukes won the first game 3–2. In the second game, the Heroes beat the Dukes 1–0. Shocked by their first loss of the season, the Dukes lost the third game 4–1.

"I thought we'd win three straight games," Dukes' Coach Matt Johnson said.

The Heroes were scoreless in the fourth game, giving the Dukes an easy win. The teams were even-steven heading into the fifth game: Each team had won two games. The team that won the fifth game would win the city championship.

The Heroes showed up ready to play. They scored two runs in the first inning. The Dukes scored in the second inning, but that was it for the Dukes. The Heroes went on to win the game by four runs.

"What a day!" Coach Lynd said. "Our season started out a little rough. But the kids pulled together and played really well. I'm very proud of every one of the players."

Josh Hampton steps up to the plate for the Heroes.

| Harvey's Heroes | 5 |
| Dylan's Dukes | 1 |

Newspaper Article

Read the selection. Then complete this page.

1. Andy and Trevor broke their arms in the same baseball game.
   - Ⓐ true   Ⓑ false

2. Which player was picked to be the new pitcher?
   - Ⓐ Andy Vann   Ⓒ Tony Valdez
   - Ⓑ Trevor Benson   Ⓓ Harvey Sanders

3. Who is Ty Gregg?
   - Ⓐ the new catcher
   - Ⓑ the catcher who broke his arm
   - Ⓒ the sponsor of Dylan's Dukes
   - Ⓓ the reporter who wrote the article

4. What can you guess from this article?
   - Ⓐ Trevor would rather skateboard than play baseball.
   - Ⓑ The Heroes' players and coach make a good team.
   - Ⓒ The Heroes always win the city tournament.
   - Ⓓ All of the people in Hometown, NY, love baseball.

5. When did Andy break his arm?
   - Ⓐ during the first game
   - Ⓑ before the season even started
   - Ⓒ before the first game
   - Ⓓ in the championship game

6. Which of these is an opinion?
   - Ⓐ All of the players love to play baseball.
   - Ⓑ Harvey's Heroes won the tournament.
   - Ⓒ Ira Douglas closed his business and moved to Florida.
   - Ⓓ Harvey Sanders agreed to sponsor the team.

7. What is the purpose of the article?
   - Ⓐ to teach you how to play baseball
   - Ⓑ to tell the history of baseball
   - Ⓒ to make you want to eat at Harvey's Sub Shop
   - Ⓓ to tell who won the city baseball championship

8. In the sentence "**The teams were even-steven** heading into the fifth game," the boldfaced phrase means
   - Ⓐ both teams have a player named Steven
   - Ⓑ the Dukes had scored seven runs
   - Ⓒ both teams had won two games
   - Ⓓ both teams had won five games

9. What is the main idea of the article?
   - Ⓐ The Heroes' season started out rough, but they became the city champions.
   - Ⓑ It was hard for the Heroes to beat the Dukes in the city championship.
   - Ⓒ Andy Vann broke his arm, so the team did not have a pitcher.
   - Ⓓ Coach Lynd is a good coach.

10. In this article, the word *season* means
    - Ⓐ to add flavor with salt or pepper
    - Ⓑ the part of the year when baseball games are played
    - Ⓒ one of the four natural parts of the year
    - Ⓓ a time when fruit is ready to pick

11. According to the article, why does Coach Lynd think the Heroes won?
    - Ⓐ They scored two runs in the first inning.
    - Ⓑ They swept the first team they played.
    - Ⓒ Harvey Sanders loves baseball.
    - Ⓓ The players pulled together and played really well.

12. The Heroes had to beat the Dukes three times to win the championship.
    - Ⓐ true
    - Ⓑ false

Newspaper Article

Use the passage to determine the order in which the events took place. Number the statements from 1 to 12 to show the correct order.

☐ The Heroes win the championship.

☐ The pitcher, Andy Vann, breaks his arm.

☐ Tony Valdez becomes the team's pitcher.

☐ Ira closes the Ice Palace.

☐ The catcher, Trevor Benson, breaks his arm.

☐ The Dukes lose the third game 4–1.

☐ The Heroes' fans think the season is over.

☐ Josh Hampton becomes the team's catcher.

☐ The Heroes beat the Dukes by four runs.

☐ Harvey Sanders becomes the team sponsor.

☐ The Heroes win all three games in the first round of the playoffs.

☐ The Heroes beat the Colts in the second round of the playoffs.

Office Ox

Stomping out high prices on office supplies

High Prices

Buy One, Get One Free

Perfect Point washable markers

Ten-pack
- Bold, bright, and pastel colors
- Quick drying
- Retractable— no more lost caps!

Limit: three free packs

You pay $89*!

Number Cruncher A+ Science Calculator Model #A793

- Red or blue case
- Computer cable included

*Regular price $129. Sale price is based on $20-off coupon below plus $20 mail-in rebate. Visit one of our stores for more details.

Paper Pride one-subject notebooks 69¢

- College or wide ruled
- 100 sheets

Regular price $1.29
Limit: ten

50% off select Paper Pal products

Clearance binders, folders, notebooks, and more

Supplies are limited. Items vary by store location.

CopyCat 50-pack CD-Rs $3.25

While supplies last!
Wow! Save 75%!

Regular price $13

Fold 'n' Find folders 26¢ each

- Two pockets
- Assorted colors

No limit.
Not available online.

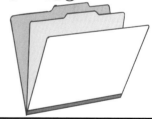

Visit all Five of our Locations

1193 Grant Street
7911 Payne Avenue
719 W. Connor Way
249 Craig Court
1760 Clark Center
Coming Soon! Our newest store at
2580 Main Street

$20 off any purchase of $100 or more!

Office Ox Store Coupon
Valid this week only!

Discounts valid this week only!
Shop online at officeox.web
Some sale items are not available online.

Valid only at Office Ox. Visit one of our stores for more details.

Name _____ Date _____

Read the selection. Then complete this page.

1. According to the ad, which of these is 50% off?
   - (A) Fold 'n' Find folders
   - (B) select Paper Pal products
   - (C) Paper Pride notebooks
   - (D) Number Cruncher calculator

2. The sales in this ad are valid for
   - (A) six months
   - (B) two weeks
   - (C) one week
   - (D) three days

3. The $20.00 coupon might be used for which of these products?
   - (A) Number Cruncher calculator, $129.00
   - (B) portable phone system, $49.00
   - (C) three packs of CopyCat CD-Rs, $3.25 each
   - (D) inkjet printer, $85.99

4. If you buy two packs of Perfect Point washable markers, how many free packs will you get?
   - (A) 3
   - (B) 1
   - (C) 2
   - (D) 4

5. How can a person save $40.00 on the calculator?
   - (A) by buying it this week
   - (B) by sending in the mail-in rebate
   - (C) by using the $20.00 coupon
   - (D) by using the coupon and sending in the mail-in rebate

6. Which of these has a limit of ten?
   - (A) Paper Pride notebooks
   - (B) Number Cruncher calculator
   - (C) Fold 'n' Find folders
   - (D) Perfect Point washable markers

7. Office Ox is the best place to buy paper products.
   - (A) fact
   - (B) opinion

8. In this ad, *valid* means
   - (A) not expensive
   - (C) hard to find
   - (B) expensive
   - (D) in effect

9. Which statement can you infer from the ad?
   - (A) Perfect Point markers are the best markers.
   - (B) You will never lose a Perfect Point marker.
   - (C) Perfect Point markers do not have caps.
   - (D) You can always get a free pack of Perfect Point markers.

10. For which of the following items is the price not listed?
    - (A) Copy Cat 50-pack CD-Rs
    - (B) Fold 'n' Find folders
    - (C) Perfect Point washable markers
    - (D) Number Cruncher A+ Science Calculator

11. If you do not want to go to the store, you can purchase any sale item online.
    - (A) true
    - (B) false

12. Which of the following is most likely to also be one of the Paper Pal products on sale for 50% off?
    - (A) loose-leaf paper
    - (B) computer cables
    - (C) portable telephones
    - (D) calculators

Sales Flyer

Use the selection to complete each question.

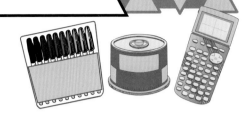

1. What do you have to do to buy the calculator for $89.00?

   _____

   _____

   _____

2. Based on the flyer, do you think you would be likely to find a basketball at Office Ox? Explain.

   _____

   _____

   _____

3. Do you think this flyer is aimed at adults or children? Explain.

   _____

   _____

   _____

4. Why do you think the store owners chose an ox as their mascot?

   _____

   _____

   _____

5. Which section of the flyer did you first notice? Why do you think that is?

   _____

   _____

   _____

6. If you had to pick a different mascot for the store, what would you choose? Explain.

   _____

   _____

   _____

Movies

Starplex 8

Hwy 21@ Rontin Rd.
555-0172

The Lucky Ticket (PG)
11:00 1:15 3:30 5:45 8:00 10:15

Dog Pound (G)
1:00 3:00 5:00 7:00

Frozen Lake (G)
11:05 1:30 4:35 7:40 10:40

Out of the Park (PG-13)
3:15 7:05 10:00

The Bionic Bunch (PG)*
11:40 2:00 4:20 6:45 9:15

Dolphin Ride (G)
11:15 1:30 4:00 7:15

Terrific Trio (PG)
10:30 1:15 4:05 7:10 10:05

In the Castle (PG-13)*
11:30 2:05 4:35 7:15 10:05

All shows before 5:00 PM are $3.50. After 5:00 PM, tickets are $6.00.

Mountain View Theatre 4

405 Canyon Parkway
555-0157
All Tickets $1.00

The Time Machine (PG)
1:00 3:00 5:00 7:00

Off the Track (PG)
3:15 6:45 9:30

Monkey Business (G)
11:15 1:30 3:45

The Party (PG-13)
3:45 6:15 9:00 11:15

Highlands Mall Cinema 5

I-12 @ Park Street exit 555-0122

Frozen Lake (G)
10:40 1:30 4:35 7:40 10:40

In the Castle (PG-13)*
10:30 1:15 4:05 7:10 10:10

Dog Pound (G)
12:30 2:30 4:30 6:30

Out of the Park (PG-13)
5:15 7:30 9:45

The Bionic Bunch (PG)*
12:00 2:25 4:50 7:15 9:40

On Sundays, tickets are only $3.00.
Tickets are $9.00 at all other times.

The Lucky Ticket

"Hilarious!"
—Beth Timer, The York News

"All Thumbs Up!"
—Albert and Hoper

starring
Tommy Bepp

Cinema 6

321 Town Center @ Loop 399
555-0182

The Lucky Ticket (PG)
11:05 1:45 3:30 5:45 8:05 10:30

Frozen Lake (G)
1:30 3:40 5:50 8:00 10:10

Dolphin Ride (G)
11:15 1:15 3:15 5:15

Dog Pound (G)
12:30 2:30 4:30 6:30

Out of the Park (PG-13)
5:15 7:30 9:45

The Bionic Bunch (PG)*
12:00 2:25 4:50 7:15 9:40

All shows before 6:00 PM—$4.25
After 6:00 PM—$8.00
All G-rated shows are $3.00.

"The Year's Biggest Thriller!"
Charles Wright—Rolling Pebble

Frozen Lake

starring
Shad Piff

Now Playing!
Starplex 8   Cinema 6
Highlands Mall Cinema 5

* Movie passes may not be used for this movie.

Name _____ Date _____

Movie Listings

Read the selection. Then complete this page.

1. What is the purpose of the movie listings?
   Ⓐ to tell which movies are available to rent
   Ⓑ to tell which theater is best
   Ⓒ to tell which movies are playing and when
   Ⓓ to tell which movies will win an award this year

2. Which is the cheapest theater to see *Out of the Park* on a Sunday afternoon?
   Ⓐ Highlands Mall Cinema 5
   Ⓑ *The Lucky Ticket*
   Ⓒ Cinema 6
   Ⓓ Mountain View Theatre 4

3. You can see *Monkey Business* for only $1.00.
   Ⓐ true
   Ⓑ false

4. Which theater is not showing *Frozen Lake*?
   Ⓐ Cinema 6
   Ⓑ Starplex 8
   Ⓒ Mountain View Theatre 4
   Ⓓ Highlands Mall Cinema 5

5. What kind of movie is *The Lucky Ticket*?
   Ⓐ suspense   Ⓒ action
   Ⓑ romance   Ⓓ comedy

6. Which theater is on Canyon Parkway?
   Ⓐ Highlands Mall Cinema 5
   Ⓑ Mountain View Theatre 4
   Ⓒ *Frozen Lake*
   Ⓓ Cinema 6

7. Which statement is an opinion about *Frozen Lake*?
   Ⓐ It is the year's biggest thriller.
   Ⓑ It is playing at the Starplex 8.
   Ⓒ It is rated G.
   Ⓓ It is playing at 1:30.

8. You want to watch *The Lucky Ticket, Terrific Trio,* and *Dolphin Ride* at the same theater. Which theater should you choose?
   Ⓐ Starplex 8
   Ⓑ Mountain View Theatre 4
   Ⓒ Highlands Mall Cinema 5
   Ⓓ Cinema 6

9. You want to watch all of the G-rated movies in alphabetical order. Which movie should you watch first?
   Ⓐ *Frozen Lake*
   Ⓑ *Monkey Business*
   Ⓒ *The Bionic Bunch*
   Ⓓ *Dog Pound*

10. What does the asterisk (*) next to a movie title mean?
    Ⓐ No kids are allowed.
    Ⓑ It's a special sneak preview.
    Ⓒ No movie passes are allowed.
    Ⓓ There will be one showing only.

11. If you wanted to use two free movie passes, which movies could you see?
    Ⓐ *Terrific Trio* and *Dog Pound*
    Ⓑ *The Bionic Bunch* and *In the Castle*
    Ⓒ *Terrific Trio* and *The Bionic Bunch*
    Ⓓ *In the Castle* and *Dog Pound*

12. What is the purpose of placing ads for movies on the same page of the newspaper as the movie listings?
    Ⓐ to convince people to buy the newspaper
    Ⓑ to convince people to stay home and rent a movie
    Ⓒ to convince people to go see a certain movie
    Ⓓ to convince people to watch movies on Sunday afternoon

Movie Listings

Use the movie listings on page 22 to complete each diagram below.

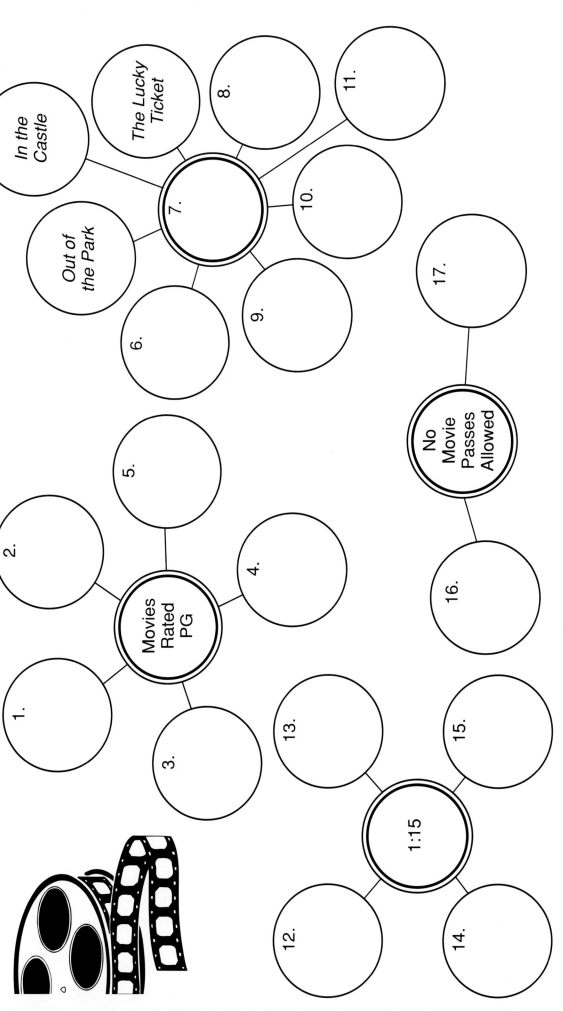

In the Castle

The Lucky Ticket

Out of the Park

7.

8.

11.

10.

9.

6.

Movies Rated PG

1.

2.

5.

3.

4.

13.

No Movie Passes Allowed

16.

17.

15.

1:15

12.

14.

Sports News for KIDS

World Series Recap and Poster

Spring Training: Where Does Your Favorite Team Practice?

David Burns Bluebirds' Catcher Will he receive the Most Valuable Player Award two years in a row?

HOMETOWN VISIT WITH ALL-STAR CARL RHODES

Alan Martinez
Tigers' Pitcher
Will Martinez's injury affect the team's season?

Dallas Dogs Cut a Deal with Coach Joe Pete Dillon

Baseball Season PREVIEW

- Major-League Baseball Team Rosters
- Draft Picks: Who Are the Best New Players?
- All-Star Interviews
- World Series Predictions
- Update on Spring-Training Injuries
- New Team Mascots

March
U.S.A. $3.95 CANADA $4.95
www.sportsnewsforkids.web

Name _____ Date _____

Magazine Cover

Read the selection. Then complete this page.

1. This magazine is written for ___.
   - (A) adults
   - (B) kids
   - (C) Little-League baseball fans
   - (D) all-star fans

2. What position does Alan Martinez play?
   - (A) catcher
   - (C) pitcher
   - (B) outfielder
   - (D) first baseman

3. Which of these would you be most likely to find in this magazine?
   - (A) football team rosters
   - (B) a hockey season preview
   - (C) a report on baseball players' injuries
   - (D) a story about a talking goat

4. What can you infer from the headline "Dallas Dogs Cut a Deal with Coach Joe Pete Dillon"?
   - (A) The team's owners made a deal with Joe Pete Dillon.
   - (B) Joe Pete Dillon played cards with the team's owners.
   - (C) Joe Pete Dillon's contract was cut into pieces.
   - (D) The team's owners like dogs.

5. Which heading announces a report about the season's best draft picks?
   - (A) Major-League Baseball Team Rosters
   - (B) Hometown Visit With All-Star Carl Rhodes
   - (C) Is Burns Hall of Fame Material?
   - (D) Draft Picks—Who Are the Best New Players?

6. This is David Burns' first year.
   - (A) true
   - (B) false

7. Which word or words could be used for *update* in "Update on Spring Training Injuries"?
   - (A) new information
   - (B) upbeat
   - (C) change-up
   - (D) research

8. Which sentence is an opinion?
   - (A) David Burns was the MVP last year.
   - (B) Team rosters and a World Series poster are featured.
   - (C) The all-star interviews are the best reports in the issue.
   - (D) The Tigers' pitcher has a sore wrist.

9. In which book could you read about Alan Martinez's pitching records?
   - (A) a book titled *Baseball's Beginnings*
   - (B) a dictionary
   - (C) a baseball almanac
   - (D) a world atlas

10. In this selection, the word *preview* means
    - (A) a look at the season before it starts
    - (B) an advertisement for a baseball team
    - (C) a movie about baseball
    - (D) spring training

11. The purpose of this selection is to
    - (A) tell readers who will win the World Series this year
    - (B) interview new baseball players
    - (C) persuade people to buy the magazine
    - (D) explain how baseball players get hurt

12. This magazine is from the middle of the baseball season.
    - (A) true
    - (B) false

Name _____ Date _____

Sort titles from the cover into the categories below.

The Players

1. _____

   _____

2. _____

3. _____

4. _____

5. _____

The World Series

8. _____

   _____

9. _____

   _____

Spring Training

6. _____

   _____

7. _____

   _____

Team Information

10. _____

11. _____

12. _____

Choose one title. Write a paragraph about it.

_____

title

_____

_____

_____

_____

_____

_____

_____

Go Fish!

Rules for two to four players

Object of the game

Try to collect four matching number cards or face cards. The player with the most sets when the draw pile runs out of cards is the winner.

To play

Remove the jokers from the card deck. Shuffle the remaining cards. The dealer gives five cards to each player and then places the rest of the cards facedown in a draw pile. Players study their cards. The player to the left of the dealer begins the game. Player 1 asks any other player for a card that will match one or more of the cards in his or her hand. For example, Player 1 asks, "Do you have any sevens?"

If the player has the requested card, he or she gives it to Player 1. If the player has more than one of that card, he or she must give them all to Player 1. Then play passes to the next player to the left.

If the player does not have the card, he or she answers, "Go fish!" Player 1 takes a card from the draw pile. Then play passes to the next player to the left.

The next player takes a turn in a like manner.

Each time a player collects four matching cards, the player places the set faceup in front of his or her playing area.

When all of the cards have been drawn from the pile, each player counts his or her complete sets.
The player with the most sets is the winner.

Kids at Play, Inc.
Check out www.kidsatplay.web for more fun card games for kids!

Name _____ Date _____

Game Rules

Read the selection. Then complete this page.

1. What is the object of the game?
   - Ⓐ to collect all of the cards
   - Ⓑ to collect the most four-card sets
   - Ⓒ to say, "Go fish!"
   - Ⓓ to collect the fewest four-card sets

2. How many players can play at one time?
   - Ⓐ up to five players
   - Ⓑ one to three players
   - Ⓒ two to four players
   - Ⓓ no more than three players

3. The player _____ takes the first turn.
   - Ⓐ to the left of the dealer
   - Ⓑ who dealt the cards
   - Ⓒ with the most cards
   - Ⓓ to the right of the dealer

4. Each player begins the game with five cards.
   - Ⓐ true   Ⓑ false

5. When might a player say "Go fish"?
   - Ⓐ at the beginning of the game
   - Ⓑ when a player has collected a set of four cards
   - Ⓒ to let everyone who is playing know that he or she has won
   - Ⓓ when another player asks for a card he or she does not have

6. According to the selection, how is the dealer chosen?
   - Ⓐ The players roll a die.
   - Ⓑ The selection does not tell how to choose the dealer.
   - Ⓒ The player who owns the cards deals them.
   - Ⓓ The players toss a coin.

7. Go Fish! is the easiest card game to play.
   - Ⓐ fact
   - Ⓑ opinion

8. The game is over when
   - Ⓐ a player uses all of his or her cards
   - Ⓑ all of the players use all of their cards
   - Ⓒ all of the cards in the draw pile have been used
   - Ⓓ a player says "Go fish!"

9. Players must keep all of their sets in their hands.
   - Ⓐ true
   - Ⓑ false

10. Which of these is a fact from the selection?
    - Ⓐ Play passes to the left.
    - Ⓑ Players need a special deck of cards.
    - Ⓒ The dealer takes the first turn.
    - Ⓓ Players collect sets of three cards.

11. What causes a player to draw from the pile?
    - Ⓐ He or she is on the dealer's left.
    - Ⓑ He or she gets the requested card.
    - Ⓒ He or she is the dealer.
    - Ⓓ He or she does not get the requested card.

12. Go Fish! is the only card game Kids at Play, Inc., makes.
    - Ⓐ true
    - Ⓑ false

Name _____ Date _____

 **Game Rules**

Use the selection to complete the page.
Number the steps in order from 1 to 11.

┌─┐
│ │   Player 1 puts her set of cards on the table.
└─┘

┌─┐
│ │   The dealer shuffles the cards.
└─┘

┌─┐
│ │   Player 2 takes a turn.
└─┘

┌─┐
│ │   Player 3 says, "Go fish!"
└─┘

┌─┐
│ │   The dealer places the rest of the cards facedown in a draw pile.
└─┘

┌─┐
│ │   Player 3 does not have any matching cards.
└─┘

┌─┐
│ │   The dealer removes the jokers from the deck of cards.
└─┘

┌─┐
│ │   Player 1 takes a card from the draw pile.
└─┘

┌─┐
│ │   Player 1 asks Player 3 for a card to match one of her cards.
└─┘

┌─┐
│ │   The dealer gives five cards to each player.
└─┘

┌─┐
│ │   The drawn card gives Player 1 a set of four matching cards.
└─┘

The *Royal Throne* Assembly Instructions

Kit parts:

A.
chairback (1)

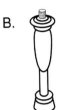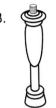
B.
chair leg (4)

C.
armrest (2)

D.
chair seat (1)

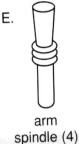
E.
arm spindle (4)

F.
package of screws (1)

G.
bottle of glue (1)

H.
sheet of sandpaper (6)

Tools needed:
screwdriver
paint and paintbrushes

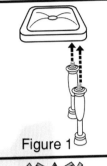
Figure 1

Figure 2

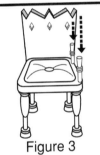
Figure 3

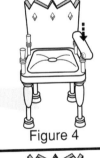
Figure 4

Finished Chair

Directions:

1. Screw two legs (B) to the under side of the chair seat (D) on the right. (See Figure 1.)

2. Screw two legs (B) to the under side of the chair seat on the left.

3. Place the chairback (A) against the rear edge of the chair seat. Screw into place. (See Figure 2.)

4. Glue two arm spindles (E) to the right edge of the chair seat. (See Figure 3.)

5. Glue two arm spindles (E) to the left edge of the chair seat.

6. Glue armrest (C) to the top of the right arm spindles. (See Figure 4.)

7. Glue armrest (C) to the top of the left arm spindles.

8. Allow the glue to dry for 24 hours.

9. Sand the entire chair until smooth.

10. Paint and decorate as desired.

Name _____ Date _____

Assembly Instructions

Read the selection. Then complete this page.

1. These instructions tell how to make
   - Ⓐ a rocking chair
   - Ⓒ a bench
   - Ⓑ a kitchen chair
   - Ⓓ a throne

2. What is the difference between kit parts A and C?
   - Ⓐ Part A is larger.
   - Ⓑ Part C is red.
   - Ⓒ Part A is never used.
   - Ⓓ Part C is oval.

3. Why must the chair be sanded until it is smooth?
   - Ⓐ It is made of wood.
   - Ⓑ It is made of metal.
   - Ⓒ It will be used at the beach.
   - Ⓓ It is old.

4. Which of the following statements is a fact from the instructions?
   - Ⓐ It will take one hour to make this chair.
   - Ⓑ The chair will look better once it is painted.
   - Ⓒ You will need a screwdriver to put the chair together.
   - Ⓓ There are seven sheets of sandpaper included in the parts.

5. Which of the following steps should be done first?
   - Ⓐ Paint and decorate as desired.
   - Ⓑ Screw two legs (B) to the underside of the chair seat on the left.
   - Ⓒ Glue two arm spindles (E) to the right edge of the chair seat.
   - Ⓓ Screw two legs (B) to the underside of the chair seat (D) on the right.

6. What is piece A?
   - Ⓐ a chair leg
   - Ⓑ the chair seat
   - Ⓒ an armrest
   - Ⓓ the chairback

7. A hammer is needed for assembly.
   - Ⓐ true
   - Ⓑ false

8. What might happen to the chair if you do not let the glue dry for 24 hours?
   - Ⓐ It might shrink.
   - Ⓑ It might fall apart.
   - Ⓒ It might change colors.
   - Ⓓ It might lose its special powers.

9. Figure 3 shows
   - Ⓐ legs being screwed to the underside of the chair seat on the right
   - Ⓑ the chairback being attached to the chair seat
   - Ⓒ arm spindles being glued to the chair seat
   - Ⓓ an armrest being glued to the arm spindles

10. What should you do right after putting the chair together?
    - Ⓐ Wait for the glue to dry.
    - Ⓑ Sand it.
    - Ⓒ Paint it.
    - Ⓓ Sit in it.

11. Which of the following is not a part included in the kit?
    - Ⓐ sandpaper
    - Ⓑ screws
    - Ⓒ screwdriver
    - Ⓓ glue

12. Why were Figures 1–4 included in the instructions?
    - Ⓐ to confuse the person who puts the chair together
    - Ⓑ to make it easier to put the chair together
    - Ⓒ to fill extra space on the paper
    - Ⓓ to give decorating ideas

Assembly Instructions

Use the selection to complete the flow chart below.

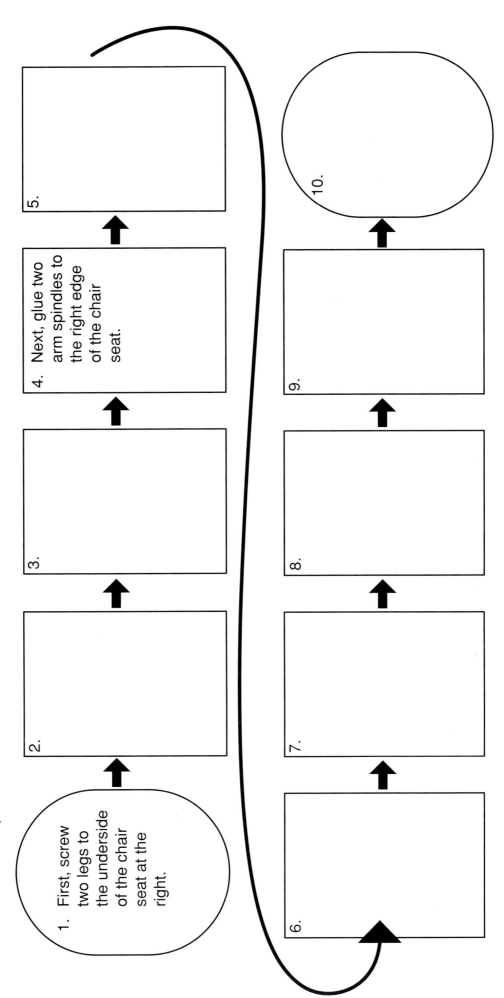

1. First, screw two legs to the underside of the chair seat at the right.

2.

3.

4. Next, glue two arm spindles to the right edge of the chair seat.

5.

6.

7.

8.

9.

10.

Real Chocolate Chips

Double Chocolate Cookies

3 c. all-purpose flour
1 tsp. baking soda
1 tsp. salt
1 c. melted butter
$\frac{3}{4}$ c. white sugar
$\frac{3}{4}$ cup packed brown sugar
1 tsp. vanilla
2 large eggs, beaten
1 c. semi-sweet chocolate chips
1 c. white chocolate chips
1 c. chopped pecans (optional)

Preheat the oven to 375°. In a small bowl, combine the flour, baking soda, and salt. Set aside. In a large bowl, beat the butter, white sugar, brown sugar, and vanilla until creamy. Add beaten eggs to the batter. Continue mixing. Gradually stir the flour mixture into the batter, mixing slowly. Blend in chocolate chips. Add nuts if desired. Scoop dough into a tablespoon. Drop dough onto an ungreased baking sheet, leaving space between each cookie. (Cookies will spread during baking.) Bake for 13 to 15 minutes. Let stand for three to four minutes. Using a spatula, move each cookie to a wire rack to cool. Serve.

Recipe makes about 4 dozen cookies.

©The Mailbox® • *Real-World Comprehension Practice* • TEC60917

Recipe

Read the selection. Then complete this page.

1. How much flour is called for in the recipe?
   - (A) 3 cups
   - (B) $2\frac{1}{2}$ cups
   - (C) $1\frac{1}{2}$ cups
   - (D) 2 cups

2. Why are the cookies moved to a wire rack?
   - (A) to keep the cookies from breaking
   - (B) to bake the cookies
   - (C) to prevent germs from getting on the cookies
   - (D) to help the cookies cool faster

3. Which of these ingredients is mixed with the salt?
   - (A) baking soda
   - (B) brown sugar
   - (C) eggs
   - (D) nuts

4. Which step comes just before putting the cookies in the oven?
   - (A) Move the cookies to the wire rack.
   - (B) Stir in the chocolate chips.
   - (C) Drop the dough onto a baking sheet.
   - (D) Serve the cookies.

5. When is the flour mixture added?
   - (A) before adding the eggs
   - (B) after adding the chocolate chips
   - (C) before adding the chocolate chips
   - (D) in the recipe's last step

6. According to the selection, the butter needs to be melted.
   - (A) true
   - (B) false

7. Why should the cookie dough be spaced apart?
   - (A) because the cookies might not cook if they're too close
   - (B) so the cookies don't spread into each other
   - (C) so the cookies won't burn
   - (D) so the cookies take less time to bake

8. Which of these kitchen tools should be used to beat the eggs?
   - (A) wire rack
   - (C) small bowl
   - (B) knife
   - (D) fork

9. Why are the ingredients listed first?
   - (A) to let the baker know how long the cookies will take
   - (B) to give the directions for making the cookies
   - (C) to help the baker know which ingredients to get
   - (D) to show that the cookies need a spatula

10. An effect of moving the cookies to a wire rack is that the recipe makes about four dozen cookies.
    - (A) true
    - (B) false

11. In the sentence "Gradually stir the flour mixture into the batter until mixed well," *gradually* means ___.
    - (A) quickly
    - (C) slowly
    - (B) immediately
    - (D) all at once

12. In this recipe, nuts are optional. *Optional* means _____.
    - (A) very small
    - (C) not required
    - (B) often
    - (D) required

Name _____ Date _____

 ## Recipe

Use the selection to fill in the missing steps.

1. Combine the flour, baking soda, and salt.

2.

3. Add eggs to the batter.

4.

5.

6. Drop the dough from a tablespoon onto the baking sheet.

7.

8.

9.

10. Serve the cookies.

Answer the questions.

11. What do you think might happen if the chocolate chips were mixed in with the eggs, white sugar, brown sugar, and vanilla? _____

_____

_____

12. If you wanted to add coconut to the recipe, in which step might you add it? Explain.

_____

_____

Burgers, Sandwiches, and Such

Basic Burger   **$2.99**
$\frac{1}{4}$ lb. hamburger with lettuce, tomato, pickles, and Dudley's special sauce

Bigger Burger   **$3.49**
$\frac{1}{3}$ lb. hamburger with lettuce, tomato, pickles, and Dudley's special sauce

Chipper Chicken Sandwich   **$3.49**
Plump grilled chicken breast with lettuce, tomato, and Dudley's honey-mustard sauce

Perfect Pita   **$3.49**
Chicken salad with lettuce, nestled in a pita pocket

Dandy Dog   **$2.19**
Foot-long all-beef hot dog on a toasted bun

Tasty Toppings   **$.29 each**
Cheese, bacon, chili, sauerkraut, grilled mushrooms, or onions (grilled or raw)

Cool Combos

Tasty Trio

Chicken salad pita, potato salad, and a large soft drink   **$5.49**

Better Than Bigger

Bigger burger with cheese, fries, coleslaw or potato salad, and a large soft drink   **$5.99**

Classy Clucker

Grilled chicken sandwich, baked beans, corn on the cob, a side salad, and a large soft drink   **$5.79**

Best Bacon Burger

Basic burger with bacon and a choice of three tasty toppings, fries, and a large soft drink   **$5.19**

Super Sides

French fries	$1.09/$1.79
Onion rings	$1.29
Coleslaw or potato salad	$1.09
Baked beans	$.99
Corn on the cob	$1.19
Side salad	$1.19

Dudley's

Drive-Through

Dash in for a Dandy Meal!

Kids' Meals

Here, Doggie!   **$2.79**
All-beef hot dog with fries or corn on the cob (Try both for $.50 extra.)

Bite-Size Burgers   **$2.99**
Two bite-size burgers (with or without cheese), fries or corn on the cob (Try both for $.50 extra.)

Great Grills!   **$2.89**
Grilled cheese sandwich, pickle, coleslaw, and baked beans

All Kids' Meals include milk.

Drinks

Iced tea	$.89/$1.09/$1.39
Bottled water	$1.59
Soft drinks (cola, lemon-lime, orange, diet)	$.99/$1.19/$1.49
Milk or chocolate milk	$.99/$1.49
Fresh-squeezed lemonade	$1.19/$1.49

Desserts

Milk shake (vanilla or chocolate)	$1.79 (10 oz.)/$2.29 (15 oz.)
Ice-cream cone (vanilla or chocolate)	$1.59
Pie (cherry, blueberry, or apple)	$1.49
Brownie sundae (vanilla or chocolate ice cream)	$2.49
Cheesecake	$1.99

Name _____   Date _____

Read the selection. Then complete this page.

1. In which section will you find a Dandy Dog and a Perfect Pita?
   Ⓐ Cool Combos
   Ⓑ Burgers, Sandwiches, and Such
   Ⓒ Super Sides
   Ⓓ Kids' Meals

2. The statement "Dudley's Drive-Through serves tasty food" is a fact.
   Ⓐ true   Ⓑ false

3. Why do you think the food items are grouped into sections?
   Ⓐ to put similarly priced items together
   Ⓑ to make the board attractive
   Ⓒ to make it easier to find wanted items on the menu
   Ⓓ to put the higher-priced items on top

4. What can you conclude from the "Burgers, Sandwiches, and Such" section?
   Ⓐ Tasty Toppings will be added for an extra price.
   Ⓑ Most people buy burgers at Dudley's Drive-Through.
   Ⓒ Toppings are included at no extra charge.
   Ⓓ The Basic Burger is the best deal.

5. The purpose of listing two prices for a milk shake is
   Ⓐ to find out how much customers will pay for a shake
   Ⓑ to charge different prices for vanilla and chocolate
   Ⓒ to add special toppings to the more expensive shake
   Ⓓ to show the price for each shake size

6. How is the Bigger Burger like the Better Than Bigger combo?
   Ⓐ Both include side items.
   Ⓑ Both burgers are one-third pound.
   Ⓒ Both include a drink.
   Ⓓ They are the same price.

7. According to the selection, the only combo meal with topping choices is the Best Bacon Burger.
   Ⓐ true
   Ⓑ false

8. Which of the following best describes Dudley's Drive-Through?
   Ⓐ tasty and sweet
   Ⓑ quick and inexpensive
   Ⓒ warm and sweet
   Ⓓ healthy and filling

9. In the Classy Clucker combo, *clucker* means which of the following:
   Ⓐ The worker will make clucking noises when it is ordered.
   Ⓑ The sandwich is not very tasty.
   Ⓒ The sandwich is made mainly of chicken.
   Ⓓ The baked beans, corn, and salad make it a better meal.

10. What would be another good name for this drive-through restaurant?
   Ⓐ Dudley's Snacks
   Ⓑ Dudley's Burgers
   Ⓒ Dudley's Treats
   Ⓓ Dudley's Fast Food

11. Which of the following word pairs is most like the pair below?
   hamburger : Bigger Burger
   Ⓐ hot dog : Tasty Trio
   Ⓑ grilled chicken : Great Grills!
   Ⓒ chicken sandwich : Classy Clucker
   Ⓓ hamburger : Dandy Dog

12. What items do the "Cool Combos" have in common?
   Ⓐ french fries
   Ⓑ potato salad
   Ⓒ baked beans
   Ⓓ soft drinks

Name _____ Date _____

Drive-Through Menu

Use the selection to answer each question. Then write your answer in a complete sentence.

1. How are the Chipper Chicken Sandwich and the Classy Clucker different?

   _____

   _____

   _____

   _____

2. Choose one "Cool Combo" and write a new description for the menu.

   _____

   _____

   _____

   _____

3. List the desserts from your most favorite to least favorite.

   _____

   _____

   _____

   _____

4. Would you be more likely to order a combo or several separate items? Explain.

   _____

   _____

   _____

   _____

   _____

5. In which section besides desserts could milk shakes be listed? Explain.

   _____

   _____

   _____

6. Which combo would you recommend to others? Explain.

   _____

   _____

   _____

   _____

7. Name two side items that you might order. Why?

   _____

   _____

   _____

   _____

8. If you were hired to design a new menu board for Dudley's Drive-Through, what would you change? Explain.

   _____

   _____

   _____

   _____

Dudley's

Unfrosted Strawberry

Nutrition Facts

Serving Size	1 Pastry (52 g)
Servings per Container	6

Amount Per Serving

Calories:	200	•	Calories from fat:	50

	% Daily Value
Total Fat 5 grams (g)	8%
Saturated Fat 1.5g	8%
Cholesterol 0mg	0%
Sodium 180mg	8%
Total Carbohydrate 32g	11%
Dietary Fiber less than 1g	2%
Sugars 15g	
Protein 2g	

Vitamins and Minerals:

Vitamin A	12%	•	Vitamin C	0%	•	Iron	10%
Niacin	10%	•	Thiamin	10%	•	Vitamin B$_6$	10%
Calcium	0%	•	Riboflavin	10%	•	Folic Acid	20%
Phosphorus	4%						

* Percent Daily Values are based on a 2,000 calorie diet. Your daily values may be higher or lower depending on your calorie needs:

Daily Recommended Amount	Calories:	2,000	2,500
Total Fat	Less than	65g	80g
Saturated Fat	Less than	20g	25g
Cholesterol	Less than	300mg	300mg
Sodium	Less than	2,400mg	2,400mg
Total Carbohydrate		300g	375g
Dietary Fiber		25g	30g
Calories per gram:	Fat 9 • Carbohydrates 4 • Protein 4		

Ingredients: Enriched wheat flour, corn syrup, dextrose, water, soybean and other oils, cornmeal, salt, dried strawberries, baking soda, cornstarch, artificial colors, vitamins, folic acid.

Comments or Questions?
Distributed by Breakfast Bounty, P.O. Box 1233, Memphis, TN

6
TOASTER
PASTRIES
Net Wt. 11 oz.
(312 g)

Name _____ Date _____

Food Nutrition Label

Read the selection. Then complete this page.

1. In *Saturated Fat 1.5 g,* what is *g* an abbreviation for?
   Ⓐ grams
   Ⓑ grains
   Ⓒ gross
   Ⓓ great

2. If the total fat were increased from 5g to 10g, what would happen to the daily value percentage?
   Ⓐ It would increase.
   Ⓑ It would decrease.
   Ⓒ It would stay the same.
   Ⓓ It would disappear.

3. Which of the following statements is an opinion?
   Ⓐ Each pastry has 32g of carbohydrates.
   Ⓑ Baking soda is not an ingredient in the pastries.
   Ⓒ There are not enough vitamins in one pastry.
   Ⓓ Breakfast Bounty distributes the pastries.

4. If the ingredients are listed in order from greatest amount to least amount used in the pastries, which ingredient was used the least?
   Ⓐ enriched wheat flour
   Ⓑ dried strawberries
   Ⓒ dextrose
   Ⓓ folic acid

5. How many Tasty Tarts are in one serving?
   Ⓐ one
   Ⓑ two
   Ⓒ three
   Ⓓ four

6. How many servings are there in each box?
   Ⓐ four
   Ⓑ five
   Ⓒ six
   Ⓓ seven

7. Artificial colors might have been added to the Tasty Tarts to _____.
   Ⓐ make them look better
   Ⓑ make them smell better
   Ⓒ make them taste better
   Ⓓ make them feel better

8. There are only 2g of _____ in each serving.
   Ⓐ vitamin A
   Ⓑ vitamin C
   Ⓒ fat
   Ⓓ protein

9. A nutrition label lists ingredients and vitamins found in a food item.
   Ⓐ true
   Ⓑ false

10. If you had a comment or question about this product, who would you contact?
    Ⓐ Memphis, TN
    Ⓑ Breakfast Bounty
    Ⓒ Toaster Pastries USA
    Ⓓ carbohydrates

11. The ingredients listed are for strawberry Tasty Tarts. What ingredient would change for blueberry Tasty Tarts?
    Ⓐ dried strawberries
    Ⓑ folic acid
    Ⓒ corn syrup
    Ⓓ dextrose

12. Tasty Tarts have more vitamin A than any other vitamin listed on the label.
    Ⓐ true
    Ⓑ false

Name _____ Date _____

Food Nutrition Label

Use the selection to complete each chart below.

1. _____

2. _____

3. _____

4. _____

5. _____

6. _____

7. _____

8. _____

	1 Pastry (52 g)
Servings per Container	6

Amount Per Serving

Calories:	200	•	Calories from fat:	50

	% Daily Value
Total Fat 5 grams (g)	**8**%
Saturated Fat 1.5g	**8**%
0mg	**0**%
Sodium 180mg	**8**%
Total Carbohydrate 32g	**11**%
Dietary Fiber less than 1g	**2**%
Sugars 15g	
2g	

Vitamin A	12%	•	Vitamin C	0%	•	Iron	10%
Niacin	10%	•	Thiamin	10%	•	Vitamin B$_6$	10%
Calcium	0%	•	Riboflavin	10%	•	Folic Acid	20%
Phosphorus	4%						

* Percent Daily Values are based on a 2,000 calorie diet. Your daily values may be higher or lower depending on your calorie needs:

		Calories:	2,000	2,500
Total Fat	Less than		65g	80g
Saturated Fat	Less than		20g	25g
Cholesterol	Less than		300mg	300mg
Sodium	Less than		2,400mg	2,400mg
Total Carbohydrate			300g	375g
Dietary Fiber			25g	30g
Calories per gram:	Fat 9	•	Carbohydrates 4	• Protein 4

Enriched wheat flour, corn syrup, dextrose, water, soybean and other oils, cornmeal, salt, dried strawberries, baking soda, cornstarch, artificial colors, vitamins, folic acid.

Distributed by Breakfast Bounty, P.O. Box 1233, Memphis, TN

9. Of the items listed above, circle any that you think are not good for you to eat.
10. Of the items listed above, draw a star next to any that you think are good for you to eat.

Nutrition Terms I Have Heard of Before	Nutrition Terms I Have Not Heard of Before

Traditional Summer Camp Weeks
June 11–16, July 2–7, and July 16–21

One-Week Wonders
Theme Camps
All the fun of traditional camp with a twist!

Splashdown   June 18th–23rd

Make a splash with a week of water action! Take swimming lessons. Enjoy water games and contests centered around the lake. Create bubble art.

World Travelers   June 25th–30th

Take a trip around the world! Join special guests as they share pictures and stories from faraway lands. Enjoy snacks, make crafts, and play games from distant countries.

Castle Keepers   July 9th–14th

Enter a world of knights and jesters, kings and queens! Create a long-gone world with arts and crafts, games, contests, costumes, and a royal castle!

We're Out of Here!   July 23rd–28th

Enjoy the great outdoors as never before. Trek through the woods and explore the outdoors. Learn about nature photography. (We provide the cameras.) Make crafts. You can even go fishing with a homemade pole.

$320 per week

Welcome to Camp for Kids

Hike the mountains, stay in rustic cabins, splash in mountain streams, and build lasting memories. Choose from many activities: arts and crafts, swimming, archery, basketball, canoeing, games, hiking, exploring nature, and much more. Camp for Kids is the perfect place to make lifelong friends.

Each weekly session runs from Sunday—Friday. Sign in begins Sunday at 3:00 PM, and camp concludes Friday at 1:00 PM.

Bring:
blanket
twin sheet set and pillow
sweatshirt
clothes for six fun-filled days
extra shoes, socks
pajamas
swimsuit
towels, washcloths
toiletries
flashlight
bug spray
sunscreen
plastic water bottle
spending money

Camp Life

Separate cabins for boys and girls surround the large dining hall. Sports fields, a lake, a craft cabin, and a gym form the ideal setting for kids in grades 3–8 to enjoy camp life. Each staff member is chosen for his or her talent as a leader. Each member of our staff teaches camp skills and loves kids. Most staffers return year after year. We strive to provide an upbeat and safe camp.

©The Mailbox® • *Real-World Comprehension Practice* • TEC60917

Camp for Kids
Lake Lawrence, New York
Overnight camps for kids in grades 3–8

Contact us: 123-555-0134 or email info@coolestcampsforkids.web
Visit us on the Web at **www.coolestcampsforkids.web**

Did you know?

- We've been a cool place for campers since 1979.
- We've received five stars from Cool Camps, Inc.
- *Summer Days* magazine rated us the best camp on the East Coast.
- We're located in the Adirondack Mountains—just a quick trip from New York City.

Summer Camp Brochure

Read the selection. Then complete this page.

1. The best ways to contact Camp for Kids are by ___.
   - (A) letter or fax
   - (C) email or fax
   - (B) phone or email
   - (D) fax or phone

2. According to the selection, a magazine claims that Camp for Kids is the best in the country.
   - (A) true
   - (B) false

3. According to the selection, about how long has the camp been operating?
   - (A) about 10 years
   - (B) since last year
   - (C) since it received five stars
   - (D) more than 20 years

4. What do the One-Week Wonder theme camps have in common?
   - (A) Campers will create art or do crafts.
   - (B) Water activities will be enjoyed.
   - (C) Special guests will visit camp.
   - (D) Campers will take hikes.

5. If you want to explore nature, which camp is best for you?
   - (A) World Travelers
   - (B) Castle Keepers
   - (C) We're Out of Here!
   - (D) Splashdown

6. Campers that dream of visiting other countries would probably enjoy _____ camp.
   - (A) World Travelers
   - (B) Castle Keepers
   - (C) We're Out of Here!
   - (D) Splashdown

7. Why do you think a sweatshirt is listed as an item to bring to camp?
   - (A) At times, it rains at Camp for Kids.
   - (B) Nights are always cool.
   - (C) You may choose to paint a shirt at the craft cabin.
   - (D) There may be cool nights.

8. According to the "Camp Life" section, most staff members have many years experience as leaders.
   - (A) true
   - (B) false

9. According to this selection, what is true about arts and crafts?
   - (A) Arts and crafts are only offered during the Castle Keepers week.
   - (B) Arts and crafts can only be completed in the craft cabin.
   - (C) Campers can choose to do arts and crafts.
   - (D) Campers must do arts and crafts.

10. Which of the following statements is a fact about Camp for Kids?
    - (A) Camp for Kids is a cool camp.
    - (B) Everyone loves Camp for Kids.
    - (C) Camp for Kids costs $320 per week.
    - (D) Camp for Kids' rustic cabins are the cleanest in the state.

11. What is an effect of having each camper bring the listed items?
    - (A) The camper has to go shopping before coming to camp.
    - (B) The camper plans ahead.
    - (C) The camper will not lose any items at camp.
    - (D) The camper has items he needs at camp.

12. Only campers with cameras can attend the We're Out of Here! theme camp.
    - (A) true
    - (B) false

Name _____   Date _____

Summer Camp Brochure

Use the selection to complete this page.

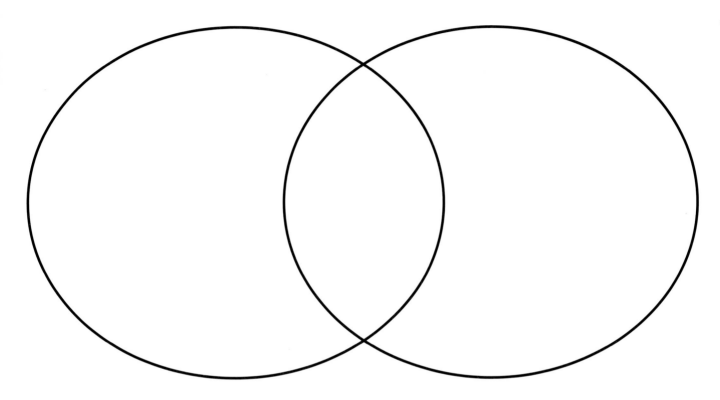

1. Use the Venn diagram to compare and contrast the Splashdown and the We're Out of Here! theme camps.

2. List two facts found in the "Welcome to Camp for Kids" section.

   _____

   _____

3. What is an opinion found in the "Did You Know?" section?

   _____

   _____

4. If you could not send an email to Camp for Kids or visit its Web site, how might you find out more about the camp?

   _____

   _____

5. On the back of this page, draw a map of Camp for Kids using the details found in the camp brochure.

GoKids.web
The ultimate Web site for kids!

| Entertainment | Games | Brainteasers | Sports | For Parents |

Can't find what you need? **Search GoKids** [   ] Go

GoEntertainment

Movie Reviews
Add your own comments about the top movies.

Celeb Shot
Learn the scoop about your favorite celebrity.

GoGames

Arcade Games
Join others in playing old and new arcade games.

Clues and Hints
Break the code and win the game!

GoParents

Homework Aids
Help your child with homework.

Web Books
Encourage reading and have access to new releases.

GoBrain

Brainteasers
Power up your brain with fun brainteasers.

Crazy Brain
Try this fun and funky game!

GoSports

Play Ball
Try your hand at classic online baseball, basketball, and football.

The News
Check the latest records and stats of your favorite players.

GoSurfing

Surf
Visit other fun kid sites on the web.

Play Online Games!

©The Mailbox® • *Real-World Comprehension Practice* • TEC60917

Name _____ Date _____

Web Site Homepage

Read the selection. Then complete this page.

1. If you cannot find what you are looking for on this page, what should you do?
   Ⓐ Play a game.
   Ⓑ Click on Brainteasers.
   Ⓒ Use the search box.
   Ⓓ Go to movie reviews.

2. Which section of the Web site is likely to have the most opinions posted by kids?
   Ⓐ GoEntertainment   Ⓒ GoParents
   Ⓑ GoGames   Ⓓ GoSports

3. What is the main idea of the GoParents section?
   Ⓐ It is a place for kids to play games and take quizzes.
   Ⓑ It is a place for kids to chat online about their parents.
   Ⓒ It is a place for parents to chat with teachers.
   Ⓓ It is a place to help parents help their kids with homework.

4. Which of these is not something you will find at GoKids.web?
   Ⓐ brainteasers   Ⓒ movie reviews
   Ⓑ sports stats   Ⓓ online store

5. For whom was this Web site primarily made?
   Ⓐ parents   Ⓒ teachers
   Ⓑ kids   Ⓓ principals

6. What will happen if you click on Play Online Games?
   Ⓐ You will go to the GoKids homepage.
   Ⓑ You will go to the online games page.
   Ⓒ You will go to the GoParents page.
   Ⓓ You will go to the comics page.

7. Laser Tag is the only game to play on the Web site.
   Ⓐ true   Ⓑ false

8. On which link would you click to find a book titled *Math Masters*?
   Ⓐ GoSports   Ⓒ GoGames
   Ⓑ GoEntertainment   Ⓓ GoParents

9. What is the difference between the games in GoSports and the games in GoGames?
   Ⓐ The games in GoSports are more exciting.
   Ⓑ The games in GoSports are sports-related.
   Ⓒ The games in GoGames are older.
   Ⓓ The games in GoGames are more challenging.

10. Who owns this Web site?
    Ⓐ Video Arcade, Inc.
    Ⓑ Brain Zone
    Ⓒ Local Schools
    Ⓓ The Education Zone, Inc.

11. What will happen if you click on GoSurfing?
    Ⓐ You will go to an online surfing game.
    Ⓑ You will go to other sites on the Web.
    Ⓒ You will go to a surf shop's Web site.
    Ⓓ You will go back to the GoKids homepage.

12. What do Music Memorizer, Laser Tag, and More Comics all have in common?
    Ⓐ They are for parents to use.
    Ⓑ They are coming soon.
    Ⓒ They are educational.
    Ⓓ They are games.

Name _____   Date _____

Use the selection to complete the site map below.

GoKids

- GoEntertainment
    - ○ _____
    - ○ _____
- GoGames
    - ○ _____
    - ○ _____
- _____
    - ○ _____
    - ○ Web Books
- _____
    - ○ Brainteasers
    - ○ _____
- GoSports
    - ○ _____
    - ○ _____
- GoSurfing
    - ○ _____

What might you add to the Web site to make it better? _____

_____

_____

The Bugle!

Announcing the best sites on the Web!

See all 218,000 results for surfing. >>

Surfing Hawaii
Check out the best spots to hang ten in the Pacific.
www.surfwaveshawaii.web

Surfer's Source
THE _surfing_ magazine! Includes travel info, contests, and more. Find out how to subscribe through the Catch the Wave link.
www.oceanlifeforme.web

Wave Catcher
This is a free site. Watch our live video cams! We focus on over 200 top _surfing_ spots. See the waves and the surfers that try to catch them.
www.catchgreatwave.web

Web _Surfing_
Surfing the Internet has never been more fun! Find everything you need with just one click of the mouse.
www.websurfing.web

Surf the Point!
Surf ten of the world's best _surfing_ spots without leaving home! Our free site offers live video cam and fun games. Join the Surf's Up Club.
www.playtosurf.web

Number One Surfer
I love _surfing!_ From Laird to Kelly, I list my favorite surfers of all time. These guys are crazy and fun to watch!
www.numberonesurfer.web

Pint-Size Surfers
Check out wave-curling kids in action! This great _surfing_ guide for kids includes a beginner's guide and safety tips. Play games.
www.kidssurf.web

Stay Safe, Surf Smart
Stay Safe, Surf Smart is a public service of the Academy of Surf and Sea. Included are links to _surfing_ product recalls and safety tips. Articles by a well-known newspaper…
www.surfsafe.web

Channel _Surfing_
Whether you have cable or a satellite dish, find the most recent movies and shows on television.
www.surfthechannels.web

last Page 1 2 3 4 5 next

Internet Search Screen

Read the selection. Then complete this page.

1. Why is the word *surfing* highlighted in each entry?
   - (A) because surfing is a sport
   - (B) because people like surfing the web
   - (C) because someone is looking for sites about surfing
   - (D) because someone misspelled the word *surfing*

2. If you wanted to learn about surfing in the ocean, which two sites will probably not help you?
   - (A) Surfing Hawaii and Surfer's Source
   - (B) Web Surfing and Surf the Point!
   - (C) Stay Safe, Surf Smart and Surfer's Travel Board
   - (D) Web Surfing and Channel Surfing

3. Which Web site tells what a fan thinks about famous surfers?
   - (A) Surfer's Source
   - (B) Web Surfing
   - (C) Pint-Size Surfers
   - (D) Number One Surfer

4. Why are the six Web sites listed on the right side of the page?
   - (A) They are not real Web sites.
   - (B) They sponsor, or pay money to, The Bugle.
   - (C) They are not related to surfing.
   - (D) They are the best Web sites about surfing.

5. Which Web site does not have videos?
   - (A) www.catchgreatwave.web
   - (B) www.oceanlifeforme.web
   - (C) www.playtosurf.web
   - (D) www.surf.web

6. The Academy of Surf and Sea runs which Web site?
   - (A) www.esurfsell.web
   - (B) www.pacificsurf.web
   - (C) www.surfsafe.web
   - (D) www.surferstravelboard.web

7. Pint-size surfers are kids who like to surf.
   - (A) true
   - (B) false

8. What do you have to do to get a free night's stay from the Surfer's Travel Board?
   - (A) Book a surfing trip today.
   - (B) Buy a subscription to *Surfer's Source* magazine.
   - (C) Write an article for the Surfer's Travel Board.
   - (D) Enter a contest.

9. What do Pint-Size Surfers and Surfer's Study Guide have in common?
   - (A) Both offer tips.
   - (B) Both offer links to clothing stores.
   - (C) Both offer games.
   - (D) Both offer trips.

10. If you want to surf in Hawaii, which is the best site?
    - (A) www.websurfing.web
    - (B) www.surfwaveshawaii.web
    - (C) www.oceanlifeforme.web
    - (D) www.surfsafe.web

11. Where can you go to sell surfing gear?
    - (A) www.kidssurf.web/shop
    - (B) www.topsurfers.web
    - (C) www.pacificsurf.web
    - (D) www.esurfsell.web/shop

12. What is the main idea of www.kidssurf.web?
    - (A) It is a Web site where kids can learn about surfing and have fun playing games.
    - (B) It is a Web site where adults can watch surfing videos.
    - (C) It is a Web site where kids can buy surfing gear for 75% off.
    - (D) It is a Web site about surfing in Hawaii.

Name _____   Date _____

Internet Search Screen

Use the selection to complete the chart. It has been started for you.

Web Site Features	
Shopping Sites	**Videos** Surf the Point!
Games Surf the Point!	**Subscribe to or Join**

Answer the questions.

1. Which site interests you most? Explain. _____

_____

_____

2. Are there more sites about surfing than those shown? How do you know? _____

_____

_____

3. What is the main difference between www.oceanlife.web/deals and www.pacificsurf.web? ___

_____

_____

Weather Map

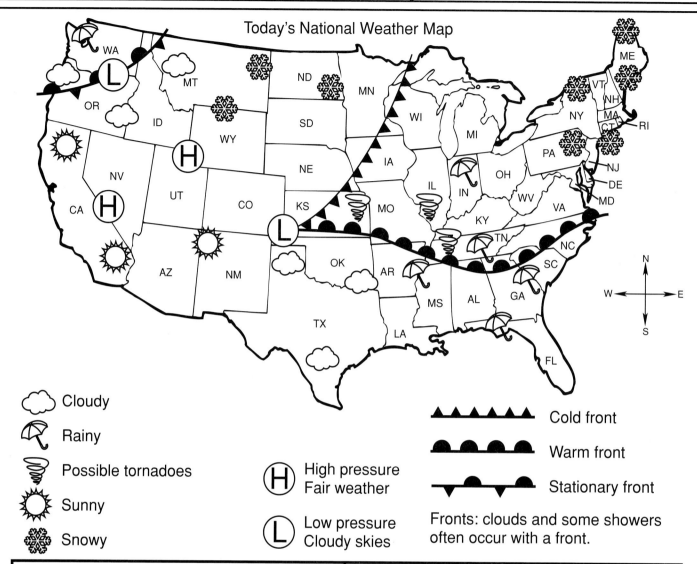

Today's National Weather Map

☁ Cloudy

☂ Rainy

🌪 Possible tornadoes

☀ Sunny

❄ Snowy

(H) High pressure Fair weather

(L) Low pressure Cloudy skies

▲▲▲ Cold front

⬤⬤⬤ Warm front

Stationary front

Fronts: clouds and some showers often occur with a front.

Midwest
A winter storm will move across the northern Midwest. The snow will blanket eastern North Dakota and Minnesota. As much as 4–6 inches of snow will fall. Ahead of the cold front, severe weather, strong storms, and tornadoes are possible across the southern portions of the Midwest. Temperatures range from lows in the 20s in the upper Midwest to highs in the 60s and 70s in the southern Midwest.

West
Weather is varied on the West Coast. In the Southwest, sunny skies and high temperatures are the result of high pressure. In the Northwest, low pressure creates clouds, and a light rain lingers. Temperatures remain cool.

South
A warm front stretches through the South to North Carolina. Severe weather is likely. There is a threat of twisters and storms north of the front. To the south, rain and warm temperatures remain.

Northeast
The cold front that moved through two days ago left wintry weather. Temperatures are below normal. Snow flurries linger throughout the northern states.

Weather Map

Read the selection. Then complete this page.

1. What is the main purpose of the weather map?
    A to show the current temperatures
    B to help people understand weather patterns
    C to show the weather over the past week
    D to show the weather forecast for the day

2. Looking at the map, what will the weather most likely be in South Carolina?
    A sunny   C snowy
    B rainy   D cloudy

3. Which of these is not shown on the map?
    A temperatures
    B weather symbols
    C fronts
    D compass rose

4. Where there is a high-pressure system, the weather is fair.
    A true   B false

5. How is the weather in Tennessee (TN) like the weather in Washington (WA)?
    A Both states have warm fronts.
    B It is cloudy in both states.
    C It is rainy in both states.
    D It is sunny in both states.

6. According to the map, what is causing the sunny weather in California (CA)?
    A clouds
    B high pressure
    C low pressure
    D a stationary front

7. Which of the following statements is an opinion about the map?
    A The map shows three fronts.
    B The northern Midwest is snowy.
    C Nevada (NV) is cloudy.
    D The map has good symbols.

8. Rain always occurs with a cold front.
    A true
    B false

9. If you are in Indiana on this day, which activity would you most likely see?
    A splashing in puddles
    B tanning in the sun
    C flying a kite
    D building a snowman

10. If you are in New York (NY) on this day, which clothes would you most likely wear?
    A raincoat and boots
    B short-sleeved shirt and sandals
    C swimsuit
    D coat and hat

11. The warm front across the Southeast may result in
    A sunshine
    B snow
    C severe storms
    D clouds

12. The key on the map helps the reader
    A draw his own symbols
    B know what the weather will be next week
    C understand the map
    D know what the weather was last week

Name _____ Date _____

Weather Map

Use the selection to complete this page. Choose the state that matches each description below.
Show the weather symbol that helps you make your choice.

Situation	State	Weather Symbol
1. You have a new snowboard and want to try it out. Which would be the ideal place, Idaho (ID) or New York (NY)?		
2. You hear tornado sirens and warnings. Where are you, Illinois (IL) or Oklahoma (OK)?		
3. You slip on your rain boots and head outside to splash around in the puddles. Where are you, New Mexico (NM) or Florida (FL)?		
4. You want to travel to where it is snowing before Thanksgiving. Where would you go, Oregon (OR) or Pennsylvania (PA)?		
5. Your school's fall picnic was canceled due to storms in the forecast. Where is your school, New Hampshire (NH) or Utah (UT)?		
6. You enjoy picturing animals in the clouds. Where would be the best place to relax and watch the sky, Wyoming (WY) or Texas (TX)?		
7. You go on an exciting adventure with your dad, who studies tornadoes. Where would your trip take you, Kansas (KS) or South Dakota (SD)?		
8. Your soccer game may be canceled due to a low-pressure system with rain showers. Where is your game, Alabama (AL) or North Dakota (ND)?		
9. Your dream vacation is skiing down the slopes over fresh fallen snow. Where should you go, Indiana (IN) or Montana (MT)?		
10. There is nothing you like better than hot, sunny weather. Which state should you visit, Nevada (NV) or Rhode Island (RI)?		

Mall Directory

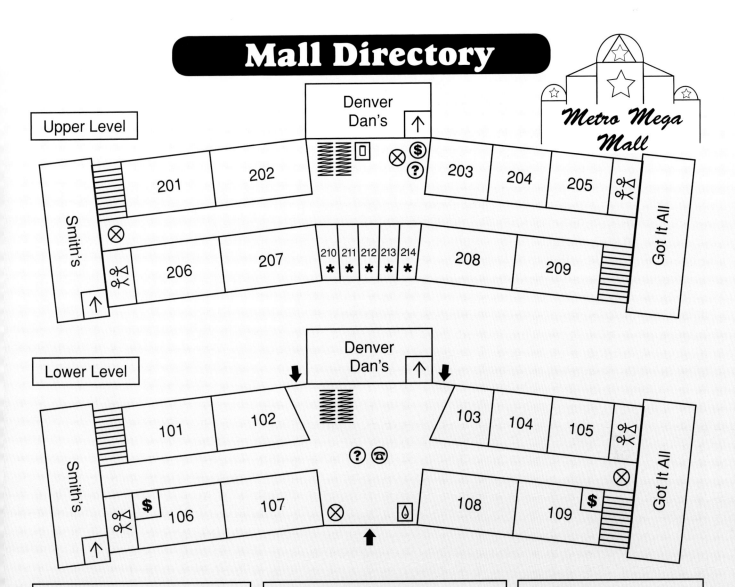

Metro Mega Mall

Clothing
101 Kiddie Closet
104 The Business Suit
205 Casual Carl's
108 Perfect Petite
107 Outdoor & More

Department Stores
Smith's
Denver Dan's
Got It All

Food/Restaurants
210 Earl's Ice Cream
211 Clever Bean
　　Coffeehouse
106 Sam's Steak House
212 Speedy Sal's
　　Sandwiches
213 Super Salads
214 Best Burger

Gifts and Accessories
207 Jenna's Jewels
204 Send a Card
209 Soap and Scents

House and Home
203 Cook's Dream
102 Fred's Furniture

Hobbies
202 Gold Medal Sporting Goods
103 Awesome Arts & Crafts
107 Outdoor & More

Personal Accessories & Services
206 Hair and There
208 Perfume Palace
105 Great Glasses
109 Picture Perfect
201 Great Nails

$ ATM
? Customer Service
▯ Drink Machines
≋ Escalator
↑ Elevator
✱ Food Court
⊗ Mall Directory
⬆ Mall Entrance
♀♂ Restrooms
▤ Stairs
☎ Telephone
♦ Water

Metro Mega Mall

Name _____   Date _____

 # Mall Directory

Read the selection. Then complete this page.

1. What is one difference between the upper and lower levels?
   A The upper level has an ATM and the lower level does not.
   B The lower level has restrooms and the upper level does not.
   C The upper level has drink machines and the lower level does not.
   D The lower level has a mall directory and the upper level does not.

2. Which store is in spot number 108?
   A Perfume Palace   C Picture Perfect
   B Perfect Petite   D Kiddie Closet

3. Which kind of merchandise is sold in spot number 108?
   A clothing   C gifts
   B food   D furniture

4. Where might you go to buy a ham sandwich?
   A Earl's Ice Cream
   B Speedy Sal's Sandwiches
   C Best Burgers
   D Cook's Dream

5. If you were shopping at Gold Medal Sporting Goods, what is the closest place to buy a drink?
   A Sam's Steak House
   B the water fountain
   C Denver Dan's
   D the drink machines

6. What is the name of the mall?
   A Got It All
   B Smith's
   C Metro Mega Mall
   D Metro Mega Mall Directory

7. Super Salads has the best salads in town.
   A fact   B opinion

8. If someone was shopping for glasses and then wanted to go to Sam's Steak House, how could he or she get there?
   A Walk toward Customer Service. Keep going straight. The restaurant will be on the left.
   B Take the stairs to the second floor. Turn right toward Smith's. The restaurant will be on the right.
   C Walk toward Smith's. Turn left at the escalator. The restaurant will be on the right.
   D Walk toward Outdoor & More. When you get to the stairs, turn right. The restaurant will be on the left.

9. What do Jenna's Jewels, Send a Card, and Soaps and Scents have in common?
   A They are clothing stores.
   B They are gift and accessory stores.
   C They are hobby stores.
   D They are department stores.

10. How many ATMs are in the mall?
    A one   C three
    B two   D four

11. Why would Outdoor & More be listed under both clothing and hobbies?
    A Because it sells both clothes and camping equipment.
    B Because it sells both camping equipment and perfume.
    C Because it sells both clothes and food.
    D Because it sells both home supplies and gifts.

12. On the map, what does the symbol ? mean?
    A Restrooms   C Customer Service
    B Telephones   D Mall Directory

Name _____ Date _____

Mall Directory

Use the selection to answer the questions below.

1. If you need to buy paints and colored pencils, in which store would you most likely shop? Explain.

   _____

   _____

   _____

   _____

2. You stop for lunch at Best Burger when you realize that you need to be at Hair and There in two minutes. What do you think is the best way to get there?

   _____

   _____

   _____

3. Why do you think that Smith's, Denver Dan's, and Got It All might be called "anchor stores"?

   _____

   _____

   _____

4. Pretend the mall is being remodeled. Which three stores would you make anchor stores? Explain.

   _____

   _____

   _____

5. Why do you think the mall directory shows only numbers instead of store names or logos? Explain.

   _____

   _____

   _____

GRANT VALLEY YOUTH CENTER
Weekly Schedule Fall Session

	Monday	Tuesday	Wednesday	Thursday	Friday
3:00	Knitting for Beginners (Classroom B)	Soccer (Fraser Field)	Hip-Hop Lessons (Classroom C)	Flag Football (Fraser Field)	Soccer (Fraser Field)
4:00			Ultimate Frisbee (Fraser Field)		Hip-Hop Lessons (Classroom C)
5:00	Volleyball (Auxiliary Gym)	Learning to Cross-Stitch (Classroom B)		Volleyball (Auxiliary Gym)	Basketball (Graham Gym)
6:00	Cooking With Cal: spaghetti (cafeteria)	Cooking With Cal: homemade chili (cafeteria)	Cooking With Cal: chicken and noodles (cafeteria)	Cooking With Cal: meatloaf (cafeteria)	Cooking With Cal: pizza (cafeteria)
7:00	Hip-Hop Lessons (Classroom C)	Cake Decorating (cafeteria)	Making Stained Glass Ornaments (Classroom A)	Basketball (Graham Gym)	Knitting for Beginners (Classroom B)
8:00	Open Gym (Auxiliary Gym)	Hip-Hop Lessons (Classroom C)	Open Gym (Auxiliary Gym)		Open Gym (Auxiliary Gym)
9:00	Dodgeball (Graham Gym)	Indoor Soccer (Auxiliary Gym)	Dodgeball (Graham Gym)	Hip-Hop Lessons (Classroom C)	Dodgeball (Graham Gym)

The Grant Valley Youth Center closes at 10:00 PM.
For more information, call 555-0134 or go to www.gvyc@acd.web

Name _____   Date _____

Read the selection. Then complete this page.

1. According to the schedule, what are the youth center's hours?
   - (A) 8:00 to 5:00
   - (C) 3:00 to 10:00
   - (B) 7:30 to 3:00
   - (D) 8:00 to 9:00

2. Which of these is offered at the youth center this week?
   - (A) hip-hop lessons
   - (C) tennis lessons
   - (B) sewing classes
   - (D) ballet lessons

3. Which activities are scheduled to last two hours?
   - (A) soccer, ultimate Frisbee, basketball, flag football, and open gym
   - (B) soccer, knitting class, hip-hop lessons, basketball, and flag football
   - (C) knitting class, ultimate Frisbee, basketball, flag football, and cooking class
   - (D) knitting class, soccer, ultimate Frisbee, flag football, and basketball

4. Which of the following is offered three times this week?
   - (A) indoor soccer
   - (B) cross-stitch lessons
   - (C) volleyball
   - (D) open gym

5. Which of these is an opinion?
   - (A) The youth center offers a variety of activities and lessons.
   - (B) The activities and lessons are always fun.
   - (C) There are many choices at the youth center.
   - (D) Activities are scheduled to begin in the afternoon.

6. Cooking classes are offered every day.
   - (A) true
   - (B) false

7. How many times are activities scheduled at Graham Gym?
   - (A) seven
   - (C) five
   - (B) four
   - (D) three

8. Which of the following activities are scheduled for Tuesday?
   - (A) dodgeball, Cooking With Cal, and Learning to Cross-Stitch
   - (B) Cooking With Cal, hip-hop lessons, and Learning to Cross-Stitch
   - (C) cake decorating class and Knitting for Beginners
   - (D) soccer, volleyball, and Cooking With Cal

9. What could you do at the Youth Center at 8:00 on Thursday?
   - (A) play ultimate Frisbee
   - (B) go to open gym
   - (C) take hip-hop lessons
   - (D) play basketball

10. How many days a week could you go to open gym at the youth center?
    - (A) two
    - (C) three
    - (B) five
    - (D) four

11. You could take hip-hop lessons every day of the week.
    - (A) true
    - (B) false

12. According to the schedule, which is a fact?
    - (A) You can learn more about the youth center at its Web site.
    - (B) At least two activities are offered every hour.
    - (C) The youth center's hip-hop lessons are very popular.
    - (D) Cal is a very good cook.

Name _____   Date _____

Weekly Schedule

Use the selection to complete this page.

1. At what times are hip-hop lessons scheduled?

   _____

   _____

2. Do you think that children who take cooking classes get to eat what they cook? Why or why not?

   _____

   _____

3. Which of the following might you be able to play during open gym: golf, basketball, or tetherball? Explain.

   _____

   _____

4. For whom do you think dodgeball is most likely scheduled: five- to nine-year-olds, ten- to 13-year olds, or 14- to 18-year-olds? Explain.

   _____

   _____

5. Which scheduled activities are arts and crafts projects?

   _____

   _____

6. Which activity most appeals to you? Explain.

   _____

   _____

Table of Contents (continued)

Chapter 4 Life Science D1
Unit 1 Plants D2
Lesson 1 Parts of a Plant D4
   Investigations*: Monocot and Dicot Seeds D7
   Life Cycles D8
   Reading Bridge*:
     Scientist George Washington Carver D12
Lesson 2 Light D13
   Investigations: Photosynthesis D15
Lesson 3 Water D16
   Mathematical Applications*: Rainfall Graph D19
Lesson 4 Soil D20
   Investigations: Soil Types D22
Lesson 5 Air D23
Unit Review D26

Unit 2 Animals D29
Lesson 1 Invertebrates D31
   Exoskeletons D33
   Social Studies Connection*:
     Lobster Fishing in Maine D35
Lesson 2 Vertebrates D36
   Fish D38
   Art Antics*: Fish Printing D40
   Reptiles and Amphibians D41
   Social Studies Connection:
     Chesapeake Bay Watershed D42
   Birds D44
   Social Studies Connection:
     Reading a Migration Map D47
   Mammals D48
   Investigations: Polar Bear Survival D51
Lesson 3 Adaptations D53
   Mathematical Applications:
     Adaptations Graph D56
Lesson 4 The Human Body D57

Circulatory and Respiratory Systems D61
Digestion and Excretory Systems D63
Muscular and Skeletal Systems D65
Nervous System D67
Healthy Bodies D69
Unit Review D72

Unit 3 Ecosystems D75
Lesson 1 Environments and Organisms D78
   Individual D82
   Population D84
   Community D86
   Habitat D89
   Niche D92
Lesson 2 Energy in an Ecosystem D95
   Investigations: Producer, Consumer,
     Decomposer D97
Lesson 3 Interdependence D99
   Food Chains D101
   Social Studies Connection:
     The Saguaro Cactus in the
     Southwest United States D104
Lesson 4 Ecology D106
   Reading Bridge: Rachel Carson,
     Marine Biologist D109
   Unit Review D111

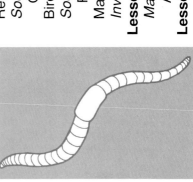

* *Art Antics*—creative expression
Investigations—hands-on experiments
Mathematical Applications—integrating math into science
Reading Bridge—content reading
Social Studies Connection—social studies links to science

Table of Contents

Read the selection. Then complete this page.

1. The table of contents is from a ___ textbook.
    (A) reading   (C) mathematics
    (B) social studies (D) science

2. On which page would you find facts about staying healthy?
    (A) D69   (C) D29
    (B) D57   (D) D72

3. What is the topic of the unit found just before the unit about animals?
    (A) air   (C) plants
    (B) invertebrates (D) ecosystems

4. Which of these statements is an opinion?
    (A) The animal unit includes facts about humans and other mammals.
    (B) The unit about plants would be better if it were shorter.
    (C) The unit about ecosystems includes information about ecology.
    (D) The plant unit lists the factors plants need to survive.

5. Why do you think a reading selection about George Washington Carver was included in the unit about plants?
    (A) Carver wrote the section about plants.
    (B) Carver built a bridge with plants.
    (C) Carver was a scientist who studied plants.
    (D) Carver drew the picture to show parts of a plant.

6. The purpose of a table of contents is to make it easier to find information in a book.
    (A) true   (B) false

7. If you wanted to find out more about lobster fishing in Maine, you might look in a
    (A) thesaurus
    (B) reading textbook
    (C) newspaper
    (D) social studies textbook

8. How do you know the table of contents is informational text?
    (A) The chapter titles tell about a story.
    (B) The information is organized by topics into sections with headings.
    (C) It lists the characters and describes the setting.
    (D) Page numbers are given.

9. Which of these is used by the author to help the reader use the table of contents?
    (A) pictures
    (B) captions under illustrations
    (C) subheadings
    (D) underlining

10. What is the purpose of the note about *Investigations* at the end of the table of contents?
    (A) Readers will understand what *Investigations* means in this table of contents.
    (B) Readers will know to complete the *Investigations* section.
    (C) Readers will be able to tell that *Investigations* and *Mathematical Applications* are the main parts of the chapter.
    (D) Readers will know that the *Investigations* sections do not need to be finished.

11. In which unit might you read about the connection between rainfall and plants?
    (A) Unit 3
    (B) Unit 2
    (C) Unit 4
    (D) Unit 1

12. The purpose of the table of contents is to persuade the reader to study more about life science.
    (A) true
    (B) false

Name _____ Date _____

Use the selection to complete this page.

1. Why do you think an experiment titled "Monocot and Dicot Seeds" is found in the lesson about the parts of a plant? Explain. _____

_____

_____

2. Why do you think *Reading Bridge* sections are included in this textbook? _____

_____

_____

_____

3. Are the pictures shown on the table of contents page helpful? Explain. _____

_____

_____

_____

4. In your opinion, what would make the table of contents easier to use? _____

_____

_____

_____

5. Which do you think would be more helpful: a review after each unit or a review at the end of the chapter? Explain.

_____

_____

_____

388 Restaurants

Granny's Fried Chicken
Since 1973

* All you can eat
Mon. & Wed. 6–8

555-0101

Alfred's Italian Restaurant
302 Highway 8 555-0198

Artie's Restaurant
4581 Main St. 555-0143

BAHAMA GRILL
4009 Valley View Dr. ...555-0156

Bueno Café
2730 Parkwood Mall.. 555-0155

Burger Queen
3032 Parker Ave. 555-0177

Chicken King
104 E. Lufkin Dr. 555-0111

Chuck D's Pizza
322 Highway 8 555-0145

Creekside Café
6220 River Parkway ... 555-0110

Darby's Seafood
7723 Crossroads St. ... 555-0123

Downtown Barbecue Pit
4102 Main St. 555-0107

Egg Roll Hut
304 Paige Pl. 555-0195

Fran's Café
3304 Main St. 555-0102

Fruitalot
2730 Parkwood Mall.. 555-0165

Granny's Fried Chicken
542 Oak St. 555-0101

Great Pizza Co., The
3085 Parker Ave. 555-0164

Hannah's Deli
4100 12th St. 555-0170

Heavenly Fresh Donuts
4320 Main St. 555-0168

Hong Kong Takeout
311 Landale Dr. 555-0118

Hutchin's Home Cooking
3005 Walnut Rd. 555-0181

I Love Ice Cream
2730 Parkwood Mall.. 555-0185

Italy Pizza
205 8th St. 555-0130

It's Delicious Deli
402 Mill St. 555-0100

It's in the Bag
356 Highway 8 555-0135

It's in the Bag
311 Cascade Lane 555-0136

It's in the Bag
5004 Main St. 555-0137

Joe's Fish Shack
302 Highway 58 555-0149

Use your local phone book.

Bahama Grill

PARTY TRAYS & CATERING AVAILABLE
TAKEOUT OR DINE IN

4009 Valley View Dr.
555-0156

The Great Pizza Co.

The Best Pizza in Town

* Thursday nights KIDS eat FREE

3085 Parker Ave.
555-0164

Name _____   Date _____

 # Telephone Book

Read the selection. Then complete this page.

1. Which restaurant has more than one location?
    Ⓐ Creekside Café
    Ⓑ It's in the Bag
    Ⓒ Burger Queen
    Ⓓ Italy Pizza

2. Which restaurant offers catering?
    Ⓐ Granny's Fried Chicken
    Ⓑ Fran's Café
    Ⓒ Bahama Grill
    Ⓓ Fruitalot

3. Which of the following is not on Main Street?
    Ⓐ Artie's Restaurant
    Ⓑ Downtown Barbecue Pit
    Ⓒ Heavenly Fresh Donuts
    Ⓓ Joe's Fish Shack

4. While shopping at Parkwood Mall, people are likely to eat at
    Ⓐ Burger Queen
    Ⓑ Chuck D's Pizza
    Ⓒ Bueno Café
    Ⓓ It's in the Bag

5. Granny's Fried Chicken has been open
    Ⓐ from 9 to 5 each day
    Ⓑ since 1973
    Ⓒ only on Mondays and Wednesdays
    Ⓓ every day since Christmas

6. If you are hungry for Chinese food, which street should you drive down?
    Ⓐ Paige Place
    Ⓑ Walnut Road
    Ⓒ Mill Street
    Ⓓ Highway 8

7. The Great Pizza Company has the best pizza in town.
    Ⓐ fact   Ⓑ opinion

8. Why is *Bahama Grill* written in all capital letters in the list of restaurants?
    Ⓐ The owners want it to stand out from the others.
    Ⓑ It is a nice place to eat.
    Ⓒ It is a seafood restaurant.
    Ⓓ It is the best place to eat.

9. How often is there an all-you-can-eat buffet at Granny's Fried Chicken?
    Ⓐ once a week
    Ⓑ twice a month
    Ⓒ twice a week
    Ⓓ every day

10. If a new restaurant called Bob's Barbecue opened, where on this page would it be listed?
    Ⓐ right before Bahama Grill
    Ⓑ right before Chicken King
    Ⓒ right before Bueno Café
    Ⓓ right after Burger Queen

11. _____ is listed right before Hutchin's Home Cooking.
    Ⓐ I Love Ice Cream
    Ⓑ It's in the Bag
    Ⓒ Hannah's Deli
    Ⓓ Hong Kong Takeout

12. Which of these is most likely to be listed on page 389?
    Ⓐ K-9 Animal Clinic
    Ⓑ Kitchen Stop Café
    Ⓒ Mike's Machine Shop
    Ⓓ Jason's Sports

Name _____ Date _____

Telephone Book

Use the selection to complete the graphic organizer below.

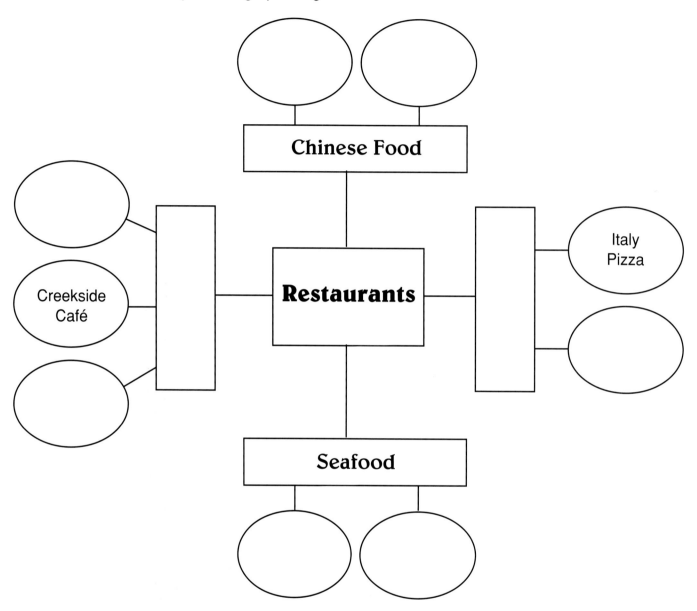

At which restaurant from the selection would you choose to eat? Explain.

_____

_____

_____

_____

Sharecropper See Farming.

Shareholder See Stock, Money.

Shark is a fish that can be found mostly in warm seawater. There are about 360 species of shark. Like other fish, sharks are cold-blooded and breathe with gills.

Most sharks have tapered bodies.

Top: Whale shark
Middle: Mako shark
Bottom: Hammerhead shark

Eating habits. Sharks often hunt and kill other animals. Different species have different eating habits. Some sharks eat live prey, and others feed on dead fish. All sharks are carnivorous, or meat-eating, fish.

Many stories tell of sharks striking humans, but there are only about 100 shark attacks reported worldwide each year.

A shark's body. Sharks come in many shapes and sizes. The smallest shark is only about six inches long. The largest may be 40 feet long and weigh as much as 15 tons. Most have sleek bodies that taper at each end. This shape helps sharks swim without using too much energy. Sharks often swim about three miles per hour, but many can swim faster for short lengths of time. Mako sharks, for example, can swim as fast as 30 miles per hour.

A shark's skin is covered with tiny toothlike scales that feel like sandpaper. These scales are often darker on top of the shark than on the bottom. This helps make the shark harder for predators to spot from above or below.

Bones. A shark has a boneless skeleton made of cartilage. Shark teeth, however, are razor-sharp and are easily replaced when one falls out.

See also: Great White Shark, Cold-Blooded Animals, and Gills

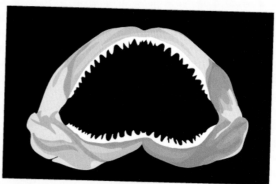

Sharks have rows of razor-sharp teeth.

Encyclopedia Page

Read the selection. Then complete this page.

1. All sharks kill their prey.
   - Ⓐ true
   - Ⓑ false

2. A shark's skin colors help keep it _____.
   - Ⓐ warm
   - Ⓑ hidden
   - Ⓒ awake
   - Ⓓ asleep

3. How does the whale shark look different from the hammerhead shark?
   - Ⓐ The whale shark has spots, and the hammerhead does not.
   - Ⓑ They both have spots.
   - Ⓒ The hammerhead shark has a tail shaped like a hammer, and the whale shark does not.
   - Ⓓ They both have tails shaped like hammers.

4. In which section would you expect to find information about the shape of a shark's body?
   - Ⓐ Eating habits
   - Ⓑ A shark's body
   - Ⓒ Bones
   - Ⓓ Shareholder

5. What is the main idea of the last paragraph?
   - Ⓐ Most sharks like to eat smaller fish.
   - Ⓑ Sharks live mostly in warm seawater.
   - Ⓒ The largest shark is almost 40 feet long and weighs 15 tons.
   - Ⓓ A shark has cartilage instead of bones and has sharp teeth.

6. What might happen if a shark's body shape were square instead of sleek and tapered?
   - Ⓐ It would swim faster.
   - Ⓑ It would sink.
   - Ⓒ It would swim slower.
   - Ⓓ It would float.

7. Why do people use encyclopedias?
   - Ⓐ to find information about a specific topic
   - Ⓑ to find telephone numbers
   - Ⓒ to find directions to the mall
   - Ⓓ to find weather forecasts

8. Which entry is most likely to appear on the next page of this encyclopedia?
   - Ⓐ Gorillas
   - Ⓑ Shareholder
   - Ⓒ Shawnee
   - Ⓓ Toys

9. Sharks are the world's most dangerous animals.
   - Ⓐ fact
   - Ⓑ opinion

10. Under which topic would you look to find information about sharecroppers?
    - Ⓐ money
    - Ⓑ stock
    - Ⓒ farming
    - Ⓓ sharing

11. If you want to learn more about sharks, under which other topic might you look?
    - Ⓐ Shoes
    - Ⓑ Great White Shark
    - Ⓒ Stingray
    - Ⓓ Bee Stings

12. Sharks often swim about _____.
    - Ⓐ five miles an hour
    - Ⓑ three miles an hour
    - Ⓒ 30 miles an hour
    - Ⓓ 40 miles an hour

Name _____ Date _____

Encyclopedia Page

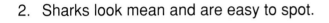

Using the selection, explain why each statement below is an opinion.

1. Sharks are very dangerous. They are real man-eaters!

_____

_____

_____

_____

2. Sharks look mean and are easy to spot.

_____

_____

_____

_____

3. Sharks and humans are a lot alike.

_____

_____

_____

_____

4. All sharks are giant predators that kill their own prey.

_____

_____

_____

_____

fes·ti·val \fes' tə vəl\ *noun* [Latin *festivus* festive]
   1: a time when people gather to celebrate, sing, and dance
   2: feast

fetch \fech\ *verb* [Old English *föt* foot]
   to retrieve or bring something back: *Will you fetch some water?*

fe·ver \fē' vər\ *noun* [Latin *febris*]
   1: an increase in body temperature: *The child's fever caused chills.*
   2: excitement or enthusiasm
   feverish *adjective*

few \fū\ *adjective* [Latin *paucus* little, *pâuper* poor]
   1: not many: *a few people*
   2: rare

field \fēld\ *noun* [Old English *feld*]
   an open or cleared area of land: *a field of corn*

fife \fīf\ *noun* [German *pfeife* pipe] a small flute

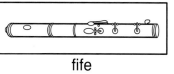
fife

¹file \fīl\ *noun* [Old English *feol*]
   1: a flat steel instrument with a rough surface used for smoothing
   2: a cardboard cover used to store papers
   3: a row of people or animals: *a single-file line*

²file *verb* [Latin *filum*]
   1: to store papers by placing them in order
   2: to march in order: *to file into the building*

fill \fil\ *verb* [Old English *fyllan* full]
   to put as much as can be held into a container: *fill the cup*

¹film \film\ *noun* [Old English *filmen*]
   1: a movie in the theater or on television
   2: a roll put into a camera to take pictures

   3: a thin covering: *a film of oil on water*

²film *verb*
   to make a movie: *film a scene*

¹fil·ter \fil' tər\ *noun* [Middle Latin *filtrum* piece of felt used as a filter]
   a device to separate material: *a water filter*

²fil·ter *verb*
   to remove or pass through a filter: *filter the sand to find small shells*

fin \fin\ *noun* [Middle English *finn*]
   the part of a fish that helps guide it through the water

fi·nal \fī' nəl\ *adjective* [Latin *finis* end]
   the last, the end: *the final game*
   finally *adverb*: *He finally reached the finish line.*

fi·na·le \fə na' lē\ *noun* [Latin *finalis*]
   the close or end of an event: *the grand finale*

fi·nal·ist \fī' nəl ist\ *noun*
   a contestant in the final round of a competition: *the two singing finalists*

finch \finch\ *noun* [Old English *finc*]
   a songbird with a short, cone-shaped bill

finch

find \fīnd\ *verb* [Old English *findan*] to come upon something after searching for it

¹fine \fīn\ *adjective* [Latin *finis*] to come upon something after searching for it
   1: nice, pleasant: *a fine day*
   2: very thin: *a fine piece of rope*

²fine *noun*
   money paid as a penalty: *to pay a traffic fine*

³fine *verb*
   to charge or make someone pay a fee: *The man was fined for the late books.*

Dictionary Page

Read the selection. Then complete this page.

1. Which word only has one meaning?
   - (A) field
   - (B) film
   - (C) fine
   - (D) file

2. Which word is most likely on the next page in the dictionary?
   - (A) fiction
   - (B) finish
   - (C) fence
   - (D) geometry

3. According to the selection, the word *file* can be used as a _____.
   - (A) verb or an adjective
   - (B) noun or an adjective
   - (C) verb or an adverb
   - (D) noun or a verb

4. Why do some words have dots between some of their letters?
   - (A) to show the meanings
   - (B) for decoration
   - (C) to show the syllables
   - (D) to show the parts of speech

5. An example for the second definition of *festival* is a banquet.
   - (A) true
   - (B) false

6. Where would the word *fifty* be listed on this page?
   - (A) after *file*
   - (B) after *find*
   - (C) before *fetch*
   - (D) after *fife*

7. Which word is a synonym for the third definition of *file* when used as a noun?
   - (A) smooth
   - (C) roll
   - (B) line
   - (D) list

8. Every entry includes a definition and an antonym.
   - (A) true
   - (B) false

9. Which word would probably be listed just before *fife* on this page?
   - (A) ferry
   - (B) finger
   - (C) flicker
   - (D) fiesta

10. Which of the following best describes the purpose of this passage?
    - (A) to argue
    - (B) to entertain
    - (C) to inform
    - (D) to persuade

11. At the top of the page, what do the words *festival* and *fine* indicate?
    - (A) *Festival* is the first word on the page and *fine* is the last word.
    - (B) *Festival* and *fine* are the most important words on the page.
    - (C) *Festival* and *fine* are both nouns.
    - (D) A festival is a fine event to attend.

12. Which of the following is included in all dictionary entries?
    - (A) examples
    - (B) the word's origin
    - (C) more than one definition
    - (D) its part of speech

Name _____   Date _____

Dictionary Page

Use the selection to complete this page.

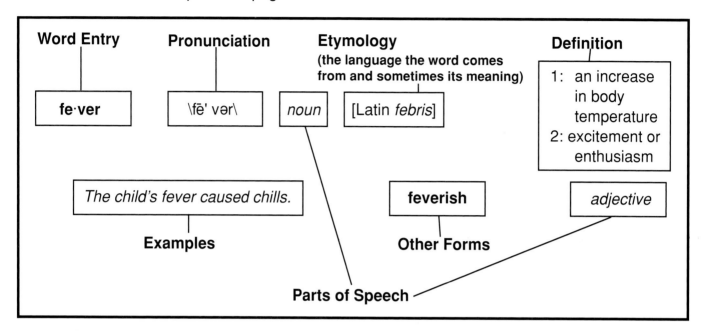

1. Write the pronunciation for the word *final.*   _____

2. What is the etymology for the word *few?*   _____

3. What is a *finch?*   _____

4. What part of speech is *fill?*   _____

5. Write an example for *festival* that might be found in a dictionary.   _____

6. Write the definition for *few* as used in the following sentence: _____
   Rainstorms in the desert are few and far between.

7. From what language does *filter* come?   _____

8. What is another form of *final?*   _____

9. How many syllables does *finale* have?   _____

10. Write the definition for *fine* as used in the following sentence: _____
    The chain was so fine that it broke easily.

Name _____ Date _____

Comic Strip

Read the selection. Then complete this page.

1. What is the purpose of the comic strip?
   Ⓐ to entertain
   Ⓑ to inform
   Ⓒ to describe
   Ⓓ to persuade

2. What ability does Lacey have that enables her to help others?
   Ⓐ She can see into the future.
   Ⓑ She can run quickly.
   Ⓒ She can stretch her arms.
   Ⓓ She can read minds.

3. Lacey did not clean her room as her mother asked.
   Ⓐ true   Ⓑ false

4. How does Lacey's mom feel when she returns home?
   Ⓐ embarrassed
   Ⓑ tired
   Ⓒ happy
   Ⓓ upset

5. Why does Lacey's mom think Lacey did not do anything all day?
   Ⓐ Lacey never listens to her mom.
   Ⓑ Lacey is on the couch, and her room is still messy.
   Ⓒ Lacey is taking a nap.
   Ⓓ Lacey is not home.

6. What happens before Lacey's mom leaves for work?
   Ⓐ Lacey messes up her room.
   Ⓑ The neighbors call for help.
   Ⓒ Lacy's mom tells her to clean her room.
   Ⓓ Lacey's mom fixes breakfast.

7. According to the selection, Lacey is lazy.
   Ⓐ true   Ⓑ false

8. How are the boy, the man, and the woman in the comic strip alike?
   Ⓐ They all live in Lacey's neighborhood.
   Ⓑ They are all part of the same family.
   Ⓒ They all need Lacey's help.
   Ⓓ They are all the same age.

9. If Lacey's mom had seen Lacey in action, what might she say to her at the end of the day?
   Ⓐ "Lacey, I wish you would do more than lay around the house."
   Ⓑ "Lacey, don't you think you could get your homework finished early?"
   Ⓒ "Lacey, if your arms were longer, you might be more helpful."
   Ⓓ "Lacey, I am proud of how much you helped our friends today."

10. How are Lacey and a nurse alike?
    Ⓐ They both are helpful.
    Ⓑ They both know first aid.
    Ⓒ They both are messy.
    Ⓓ They both enjoy the outdoors.

11. In the final scene, Lacey's problem is
    Ⓐ her mother came home early
    Ⓑ she is hungry
    Ⓒ she doesn't want to clean her room
    Ⓓ her mother does not know what really happened during the day

12. This comic strip was written for
    Ⓐ doctors
    Ⓑ school-age kids
    Ⓒ teachers
    Ⓓ parents

Name _____ Date _____

 **Comic Strip**

Use the selection to complete this page.

Cut apart the cards below. Glue each card below the correct heading.
Then answer the question.

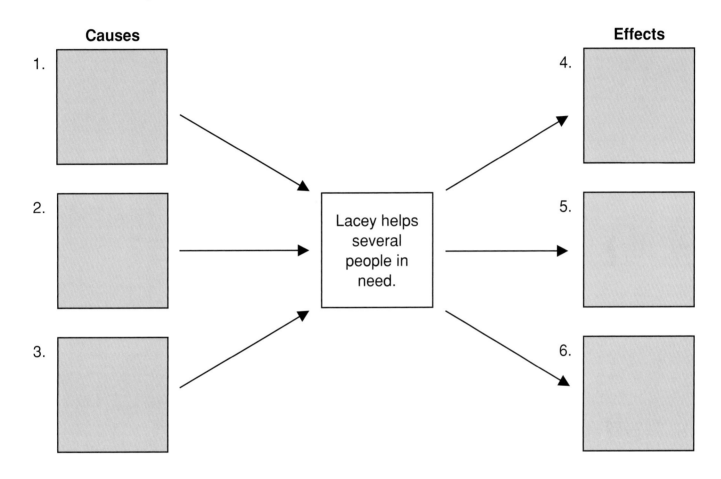

Causes

1.

2.

3.

Lacey helps several people in need.

Effects

4.

5.

6.

7. If Lacey had ignored the cries for help, what might have happened? Explain.

_____

_____

_____

_____

| Lacey is tired. | A man needs help reaching his keys. | Mom is upset with Lacey. | A woman needs help reaching her cat. | Lacey does not have time to clean her room. | A boy needs help at the park. |

Name _____

Page _____

1. Ⓐ   Ⓑ   Ⓒ   Ⓓ

2. Ⓐ   Ⓑ   Ⓒ   Ⓓ

3. Ⓐ   Ⓑ   Ⓒ   Ⓓ

4. Ⓐ   Ⓑ   Ⓒ   Ⓓ

5. Ⓐ   Ⓑ   Ⓒ   Ⓓ

6. Ⓐ   Ⓑ   Ⓒ   Ⓓ

7. Ⓐ   Ⓑ   Ⓒ   Ⓓ

8. Ⓐ   Ⓑ   Ⓒ   Ⓓ

9. Ⓐ   Ⓑ   Ⓒ   Ⓓ

10. Ⓐ   Ⓑ   Ⓒ   Ⓓ

11. Ⓐ   Ⓑ   Ⓒ   Ⓓ

12. Ⓐ   Ⓑ   Ⓒ   Ⓓ

Name _____

Page _____

1. Ⓐ   Ⓑ   Ⓒ   Ⓓ

2. Ⓐ   Ⓑ   Ⓒ   Ⓓ

3. Ⓐ   Ⓑ   Ⓒ   Ⓓ

4. Ⓐ   Ⓑ   Ⓒ   Ⓓ

5. Ⓐ   Ⓑ   Ⓒ   Ⓓ

6. Ⓐ   Ⓑ   Ⓒ   Ⓓ

7. Ⓐ   Ⓑ   Ⓒ   Ⓓ

8. Ⓐ   Ⓑ   Ⓒ   Ⓓ

9. Ⓐ   Ⓑ   Ⓒ   Ⓓ

10. Ⓐ   Ⓑ   Ⓒ   Ⓓ

11. Ⓐ   Ⓑ   Ⓒ   Ⓓ

12. Ⓐ   Ⓑ   Ⓒ   Ⓓ

©The Mailbox® • *Real-World Comprehension Practice* • TEC60917

Answer Keys

Page 5
1. C
2. A
3. A
4. D
5. A
6. D
7. C
8. B
9. D
10. A
11. C
12. B

Page 6
1. Fact
2. Opinion
3. Opinion
4. Fact
5. Fact
6. Opinion

Paragraphs will vary.

Page 8
1. B
2. D
3. B
4. A
5. A
6. A
7. D
8. C
9. B
10. B
11. D
12. D
13. C

Page 9
Answers may vary. Possible answers include the following:
Topic: Orange Grove School District's Attendance Policy
  I. Students need to be at school on time every day.
    A. Students can miss school for illness, doctor visits, family emergencies, or special holidays.
    B. Students cannot miss school for family trips or to babysit.
  II. Call the school's attendance line to report an absence.
  III. Makeup work has to be turned in within three days.

Letters will vary but should summarize the selection.

Page 11
1. A
2. B
3. B
4. C
5. B
6. A
7. D
8. C
9. B
10. D
11. C
12. C

Page 12
Answers may vary. Possible answers include the following:

Title	Price	Book	Computer Program	Audio CD	DVD	Description
1. Dandy Dinos	$5	X		X		a CD and 96-page book about dinosaurs for ages 6–12
2. Type With Tara	$5		X			a computer program that teaches typing for ages 8 and up
3. Phonics Fun	$5		X			a computer program that teaches sounds and words for ages 4–9
4. Race & Chase	$5				X	a DVD about racecar drivers for ages 6 and up
5. I Love America	$5			X		a CD with ten songs about America for ages 4–12
6. Learn Spanish	$5	X		X	X	a book, a CD, and DVD set that teaches Spanish in six months for ages 9 and up
7. Animal Adventures	$5	X		X		a book and CD about animals and zookeepers for ages 3–7

8. *Race & Chase* and *Learn Spanish*
9. *Race & Chase*
10. Answers will vary. With a computer program, you can practice typing as you learn.

Page 14
1. B
2. C
3. D
4. A
5. C
6. B
7. B
8. D
9. A
10. D
11. B
12. A

Page 15

Answers will vary.

Page 17
1. B
2. C
3. D
4. B
5. A
6. A
7. D
8. C
9. A
10. B
11. D
12. A

Page 18
12	The Heroes win the championship.
3	The pitcher, Andy Vann, breaks his arm.
6	Tony Valdez becomes the team's pitcher.
1	Ira closes the Ice Palace.
4	The catcher, Trevor Benson, breaks his arm.
10	The Dukes lose the third game 4–1.
5	The Heroes' fans think the season is over.
7	Josh Hampton becomes the team's catcher.
11	The Heroes beat the Dukes by four runs.
2	Harvey Sanders becomes the team sponsor.
8	The Heroes win all three games in the first round of the playoffs.
9	The Heroes beat the Colts in the second round of the playoffs.

Page 20
1. B
2. C
3. A
4. C
5. D
6. A
7. B
8. D
9. C
10. C
11. B
12. A

Page 21
1. You must use the $20.00 coupon and the $20.00 mail-in rebate.
2. no; Office Ox stores sell office supplies, not sports equipment.
3. adults; Reasons will vary.
4–6. Answers will vary.

Page 23

1. C	7. A
2. A	8. A
3. A	9. D
4. C	10. C
5. D	11. A
6. B	12. C

Page 24

Order of answers may vary in each diagram.

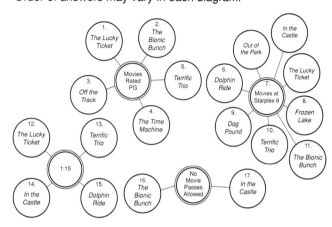

Page 26

1. B	7. A
2. C	8. C
3. C	9. C
4. A	10. A
5. D	11. C
6. B	12. B

Page 27

Order may vary.
The Players
1. Will Martinez's injury affect the team's season?
2. Will Burns receive the Most Valuable Player Award two years in a row?
3. All-Star Interviews
4. Hometown Visit with All-Star Carl Rhodes
5. Draft Picks: Who Are the Best New Players?
Spring Training
6. Update on Spring-Training Injuries
7. Spring Training: Where Does Your Favorite Team Practice?
The World Series
8. World Series Predictions
9. World Series Recap and Poster
Team Information
10. Major-League Baseball Team Rosters
11. New Team Mascots
12. Dallas Dogs Cut a Deal with Coach Joe Pete Dillon
Paragraphs will vary.

Page 29

1. B	7. B
2. C	8. C
3. A	9. B
4. A	10. A
5. D	11. D
6. B	12. B

Page 30

1. The dealer removes the jokers from the deck of cards.
2. The dealer shuffles the cards.
3. The dealer gives five cards to each player.
4. The dealer places the rest of the cards facedown in a draw pile.
5. Player 1 asks Player 3 for a card to match one of her cards.
6. Player 3 does not have any matching cards.
7. Player 3 says, "Go fish!"
8. Player 1 takes a card from the draw pile.
9. The drawn card gives Player 1 a set of four matching cards.
10. Player 1 puts her set of cards on the table.
11. Player 2 takes a turn.

Page 32

1. D	7. B
2. A	8. B
3. A	9. C
4. C	10. A
5. D	11. C
6. D	12. B

Page 33

Answers may vary.
1. First, screw two legs to the underside of the chair seat on the right.
2. Then screw the other two legs to the underside of the chair seat on the left.
3. Screw the back of the chair into place along the back of the seat.
4. Next, glue two arm spindles to the right edge of the chair seat.
5. Then glue the other two arm spindles to the other side of the chair seat.
6. Glue an armrest to the top of the right spindles.
7. After that, glue the other armrest to the top of the left spindles.
8. Let the glue dry for 24 hours.
9. Smooth the throne with sandpaper.
10. Paint the chair.

Page 35

1. A	7. B
2. D	8. D
3. A	9. C
4. C	10. B
5. C	11. C
6. A	12. C

Page 36

1. Combine the flour, baking soda, and salt.
2. Beat together the butter, white sugar, brown sugar, and vanilla.
3. Add eggs to the batter.
4. Stir in the flour mixture.
5. Blend in chocolate chips and nuts.
6. Drop the dough from a tablespoon onto the baking sheet.
7. Bake for 13–15 minutes.
8. Let stand for 3–4 minutes.
9. Move to a wire rack to cool.
10. Serve the cookies.
Answers will vary. Possible answers include the following:
11. The chocolate chips and nuts might break apart when the butter mixture is beaten.
12. The coconut is similar to the chocolate chips and nuts, so it would probably be added when they are added.

Page 38

1. B	7. A
2. B	8. B
3. C	9. C
4. A	10. D
5. D	11. C
6. B	12. D

Page 39

1. The Chipper Chicken Sandwich does not come with any side orders. The Classy Clucker is the Chipper Chicken Sandwich plus baked beans, corn on the cob, a side salad, and a large soft drink.
5. Milk shakes could also be listed in the "Drinks" section because they are drinks.
2–4 and 6–8. Answers will vary.

Page 41

1. A	7. A
2. A	8. D
3. C	9. A
4. D	10. B
5. A	11. A
6. C	12. B

Page 42

1. Nutrition Facts
2. Serving Size
3. Cholesterol
4. Protein
5. Vitamins and Minerals
6. Daily Recommended Amount
7. Ingredients
8. Comments or Questions
9. Answers will vary.
10. Answers will vary.

Chart answers will vary.

Page 44

1. B	7. D
2. B	8. A
3. D	9. C
4. A	10. C
5. C	11. D
6. A	12. B

Page 45

1. Answers will vary. Possible answers include the following:
Splashdown—water theme week, take swimming lessons, play water games and have contests, create bubble art
We're Out of Here!—nature theme week, learn photography, hike in the woods, make crafts, make a homemade fishing pole
Both camps—main activities are outdoors, sleep in cabins, make friends
2. Answers should include two of the following: campers hike in the mountains, stay in cabins, splash in streams, make friends, and choose from many activities.
3. Camp for Kids is a cool place for campers.
4. Answers will vary. Possible answers include the following: visit the camp, ask others who have attended Camp for Kids, call or write the camp for more information, read *Summer Days* magazine, and contact Cool Camps, Inc.
5. Maps will vary. All maps should include a dining hall surrounded by several cabins. The map should also include a sports field, lake, craft cabin, gym, woods, and stream.

Page 47

1. C	7. B
2. A	8. D
3. D	9. B
4. D	10. D
5. B	11. B
6. B	12. B

Page 48

- GoEntertainment
  - Movie Reviews
  - Celeb Shot
- GoGames
  - Arcade Games
  - Clues and Hints
- GoParents
  - Homework Aids
  - Web Books
- GoBrain
  - Brainteasers
  - Crazy Brain
- GoSports
  - Play Ball
  - The News
- GoSurfing
  - Surf

Answers will vary.

Page 50

1. C	7. A
2. D	8. A
3. D	9. A
4. B	10. B
5. B	11. D
6. C	12. A

Page 51

Shopping Sites
Surfing Gear
Surfer's Travel Board
Surfing
Buy Surfing DVDs and Videos
Pacific Surf

Videos
Surf the Point!
Wave Catcher
Surfer's Study Guide
Buy Surfing DVDs and Videos

Games
Surf the Point!
Pint-Size Surfers

Subscribe to or Join
Surfer's Source
Surf the Point!
Surfer's Travel Board

1. Answers will vary.
2. Yes, because the bottom of the screen shows that there are five pages of Web sites.
3. The site www.oceanlifeforme.web/deals has up to 50% off, and www.pacificsurf.web has up to 75% off.

Page 53

1. D	7. D
2. B	8. B
3. A	9. A
4. A	10. D
5. C	11. C
6. B	12. C

Page 54

1. New York; ❄
2. Illinois; 🌪
3. Florida; ☔
4. Pennsylvania; ❄
5. New Hampshire; ❄
6. Texas; ☁
7. Kansas; 🌪
8. Alabama; ☔
9. Montana; ❄
10. Nevada; ☀

Page 56

1. C	7. B
2. B	8. A
3. A	9. B
4. B	10. C
5. D	11. A
6. C	12. C

Page 57

1. Awesome Arts & Crafts because paints and colored pencils are art supplies
2–5. Answers will vary.

Page 59
1. C
2. A
3. D
4. D
5. B
6. A
7. C
8. B
9. D
10. C
11. A
12. A

Page 60
1. 7:00, 8:00, 3:00, 9:00, 4:00
2. Children probably get to eat their food because they cook it at dinnertime.
3. Golf and tetherball are outside activities so only basketball would be played during open gym.
4. Because it is always scheduled at 9:00, dodgeball is most likely for 14- to 18-year-olds. It would be too late in the day for younger children.
5. Knitting, cross-stitching, and making stained glass ornaments are arts and crafts projects.
6. Answers will vary.

Page 62
1. D
2. A
3. C
4. B
5. C
6. A
7. D
8. B
9. C
10. A
11. D
12. B

Page 63
1. Answers will vary. Answers may include that seeds are parts of a plant or that experiments help students learn about science.
2. Answers will vary. Answers may include that reading is important in all subjects or that reading will help students understand science better.
3–5. Answers will vary.

Page 65
1. B
2. C
3. D
4. C
5. B
6. A
7. B
8. A
9. C
10. C
11. D
12. B

Page 66

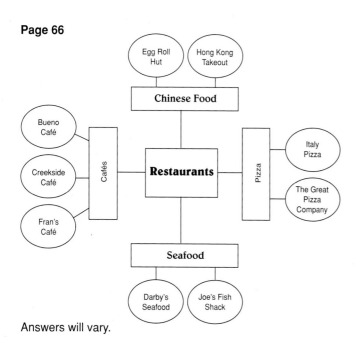

Answers will vary.

80

Page 68
1. B
2. B
3. A
4. B
5. D
6. C
7. A
8. C
9. B
10. C
11. B
12. B

Page 69
Answers may vary.

1. Sharks are very dangerous. They are real man-eaters! Some sharks do hunt and kill their prey. Many stories tell of sharks striking humans, but there are only about 100 shark attacks reported worldwide each year.
2. Sharks look mean and are easy to spot.
   A shark's skin is covered with tiny tooth-like scales that feel like sandpaper. These scales are often darker on top of the shark than on the bottom. This helps make the shark harder for predators to spot from above or below.
3. Sharks and humans are a lot alike.
   Sharks come in many shapes and sizes. The smallest shark is only about six inches long. The largest can be 40 feet long and weigh as much as 15 tons. Most sharks have sleek bodies that taper at each end. This shape helps sharks swim without using too much energy. Sharks often swim at about three miles per hour, but many can swim faster for short lengths of time. Mako sharks, for example, can swim as fast as 30 miles per hour.
4. All sharks are giant predators that kill their own prey. Sharks often hunt and kill other animals. Different species have different eating habits. Some sharks eat live prey, and others feed on dead fish. All sharks are carnivorous, or meat-eating, fish.

Page 71
1. A
2. B
3. D
4. C
5. A
6. D
7. B
8. B
9. D
10. C
11. A
12. D

Page 72
1. fī'nəl
2. Latin *paucus* little, *pauper* poor
3. a songbird with a short, cone-shaped bill
4. verb
5. Answers will vary.
6. rare
7. Middle Latin
8. finally
9. three
10. very thin

Page 74
1. A
2. C
3. A
4. D
5. B
6. C
7. B
8. C
9. D
10. A
11. D
12. B

Page 75
For answers 1–3, the order may vary.
1. A boy needs help at the park.
2. A man needs help reaching his keys.
3. A woman needs help reaching her cat.
For answers 4–6, the order may vary.
4. Lacey does not have time to clean her room.
5. Lacey is tired.
6. Mom is upset with Lacey.
7. Answers will vary.